Ae for the Mind

Practical Exercises in Philosophy That Anybody Can Do

Brenton,

I hope you enjoy these fun exercises
& learn a bit
about philosophy

Michael Pitts

June 19, 2016

Aerobics for the Mind

Practical Exercises in Philosophy That Anybody Can Do

by

Michael Potts, Ph.D.

Professor of Philosophy, Methodist University

WordCrafts

Aerobics for the Mind
Practical Exercises in Philosophy That Anybody Can Do
Copyright © 2014
Michael Potts, Ph.D.

Cover art: *Scuola di Atene* by Raphael
Cover design by David Warren

Published by WordCrafts Press
Tullahoma, TN 37388
www.wordcrafts.net

TABLE OF CONTENTS

ACKNOWLEDGMENTS

First of all, I thank Methodist University for a one-semester sabbatical that allowed me to work on this project and to the Philosophy and Religion Department, especially to the Department Head at the time, Richard Walsh. I am grateful to the members of the Methodist University Writing Group who critiqued the early chapters. The Writers' Loft program through Middle Tennessee State University and the Odyssey Writing Workshop in Manchester, New Hampshire gave me invaluable training in the techniques of good writing. I am grateful to my colleagues at Methodist University, Michael Colonnese and Robin Greene, for the learning experience in taking their courses in writing. My wife, Karen, has been patient with me during my many absences in the tiny space between bookcases in my home office where I hide out and write.

AD MAIOREM DEI GLORIAM

INTRODUCTION

WHAT IS PHILOSOPHY?

A*erobics for the Mind: Practical Exercises in Philosophy that Anybody Can Do* is a book for anyone who has a sense of wonder. One of the greatest of philosophers, Aristotle (384-322 B.C.), said that "Philosophy begins in wonder." Remember when you were a child and asked your parents "Why? "Why? "Why?" until they were red in the face. You still had that childhood gift of wondering about everything from the simple *"Why can't I touch the stove eye when it's red?"* to the most profound questions people can ask *"Why can't I see God if He's real?"* Philosophers are often considered stodgy, boring intellectuals or gurus on top of a mountain contemplating their navels - but philosophy, at its best, is a joyous profession. Philosophers never stop wondering about why the world is the way it is. They ask the most profound and universal questions human beings around the world have asked over the centuries: *"Why am I here?" "Does life have a meaning?" "Is there a God?" "Do I have an immortal soul?"* or *"What happens when I die?"* Philosophers have the joy of re-living the wonder of a child as many times as they want.

Philosophy, however, is more than wondering. It is a systematic attempt to discover the nature of ultimate reality through reason and sense experience. It is not haphazard - it is more than mere guessing. Yet it is an attempt that most often does not give us absolute certainty - rarely is there consensus among philosophers on a particular philosophical problem - though there are exceptions. For example, take psychological egoism, the view that the only motive for human beings acting in the world is their own self-interest. Thus if you see a drowning child and risk your life to save the child, your only motivation for acting that way is self interest. Although one famous philosopher of the sixteenth century, the British philosopher Thomas Hobbes (1588-1679), supported this position, it is almost universally rejected by contemporary philosophers. The reason is that defenders of psychological egoism refuse to accept any evidence as counting against their theory; rather, they interpret contrary evidence as "really" supporting their theory. For example, if you rescue a drowning child but die in the attempt, your action was not because you wanted to sacrifice yourself for another person - actually you wanted to feel good about doing it, or to look good so your boss will see your hero face on TV and give you a raise, or to avoid the guilt you will have if you fail to try to rescue the child. In this view, you were acting only from the motive of your own self-interest all along.

To illustrate the problem with this view, let us take the example of Freudianism. Freudian thought claims that boys have a secret desire to kill their fathers to marry their mothers. Suppose that you are in counseling with a Freudian for unrelated problems. The counselor tells you that you wanted to kill your father and marry your mother when you was a child. You deny that, but the counselor says, "This knowledge is in your unconscious mind, and you have repressed it."

The difficulty is that no matter what you say, the Freudian will automatically interpret your statement in terms of Freud's theory. That is not only unfair; it is an example of bad reasoning. In a similar way, a psychological egoist will automatically interpret an act that seems to be *clearly* altruistic as *clearly* self-interested. In addition, the psychological egoist does not consider the possibility that acting from a motive of altruism may at the same time fulfill a person's self-interest. For these reasons, philosophers almost universally reject psychological egoism - thus they have, in fact, gained knowledge through their reason and experience. Philosophy has standards, and like any other discipline that seeks truth, sometimes will find it.

The Major Branches of Philosophy

The major branches of philosophy are metaphysics, epistemology, logic, ethics and aesthetics.

Metaphysics is, in my opinion, the heart of philosophy - the attempt to understand ultimate reality, to understand *being qua being*. The word "metaphysics" comes from two Greek words: *meta*, meaning *after* and *phusis*, meaning *physics* - thus, *after [the] physics*. Originally the word referred to a book of Aristotle's that happened to be located after Aristotle's book *Physics* in a collection of his works. Its meaning expanded later to mean the attempt to understand reality as a whole.

Metaphysics, as the term is used in philosophy, has very little to do with the so-called "metaphysical" or "New Age" sections at bookstores. Below is a list of some metaphysical questions:

- Does God exist?
- Do universal terms such as *dogness* or *treeness* refer to anything that actually exists?
- Do human beings have a soul that can exist separately from the body?
- Is the universe ultimately one or is it many?
- Is the universe mostly changing or unchanging?

Although there have been periods in the history of philosophy in which many philosophers were hostile to metaphysics, the questions above (and many others) keep coming back. There is little danger of metaphysics dying any time soon.

Epistemology is the branch of philosophy that attempts to determine the scope and limits of human knowledge. Some epistemological questions are listed below:

- How much can we know?
- Do we know reality primarily through sense experience or primarily through reason?
- Can we reliably know anything at all?
- Must knowledge be certain?
- How is knowledge distinguished from belief and opinion?

Most philosophers use a combination of reason and sense experience to explore the ultimate questions of existence. Some philosophers prefer reason over sense experience. These philosophers are called *rationalists*. Famous rationalist philosophers include Plato (427-347 B.C.), René Descartes (1596-1650) and Immanuel Kant (1724-1804). Other philosophers prefer sense experience over reason as a means to gain knowledge. These philosophers are called *empiricists*. Famous empiricists include Aristotle, Thomas Aquinas (1225-1274), John Locke (1632-1704) and David Hume (1711-1776). Most philosophers do not side wholly with reason or experience as a source of knowledge; rationalism and empiricism are most often matters of a philosopher's emphasis rather than a philosopher being a "pure" rationalist or a "pure" empiricist.

Logic is the branch of philosophy that focuses on the rules for correct reasoning. Aristotle is the first Western philosopher to systematize logic. Today there are two kinds of introductory logic taught in colleges and universities. The first kind of logic course focuses on critical thinking and reasoning using ordinary language. It may also focus some on Aristotle's logic. The second kind of introductory logic course is often called "Symbolic Logic." It teaches a simple version of the mathematical logic developed in the late nineteenth and early twentieth centuries by philosophers such as Gottlob Frege (1848-1925), Bertrand Russell (1872-1970), Alfred North Whitehead (1861-1947) and Willard V. O. Quine (1908-2000). It is taught more like a mathematics course and emphasizes doing proofs. Advanced students can take more specialized courses in logic.

Ethics is the philosophical study of morality. While *ethics* and *morality* are often used to refer to the same thing, sometimes morality is used to refer to the specific moral codes found in particular cultures. Ethics then, would be the philosophical attempt to understand morality and determine which version of morality is best for human beings. *Metaethics* refers to a rather boring discipline which attempts to determine the meaning of ethical terms such as "good," "right," and "ought". *Normative ethics*, which is far more interesting, is the attempt to determine which rules, principles or virtues are the correct ones. *Professional ethics* refers to the ethics of various professions such as medicine or law. For example, there are medical ethics, legal ethics, criminal justice ethics, business ethics (which some people would say is an oxymoron), etc. Some ethical questions include:

- Is ethics primarily about rules, or is it primarily about a person's character?
- Should morality focus on the consequences of an action or rule, or should it
- Focus only on the rightness or wrongness of an action or rule?
- Which moral code is best?
- Is abortion morally right or wrong?

Aesthetics is the philosophical study of art and judgments about art. This includes the study of *literary* arts such as fiction and poetry as well as *plastic* arts such as painting and sculpture. Some aesthetic questions include:

- What is art?
- Is beauty in the eye of the beholder, or are there objective standards for beauty?
- Is metaphor only a decoration for language, or does it reveal parts of reality that could not be revealed in any other way?

In addition to the major areas of philosophy, there are various *philosophies of* disciplines. Examples include philosophy of religion, philosophy of science, philosophy of law, political philosophy and philosophy of sex and love. There is even a Society for the Philosophy of Sex and Love whose members gather at the national meetings of the American Philosophical Association. My wife also claims there must be a philosophy of toenail clipping, but I doubt that is the case.

A Brief Survey of the History of Western Philosophy

Ancient Philosophy

Although philosophy has a long history in the Far East in places such as India and China, this book focuses primarily on Western philosophy, which began in the seventh century B.C. in the Greek colonies of Asia Minor (modern Turkey). Philosophy began when people went beyond myth to use reason to explain the nature of reality. The ancient period of philosophy (7th century B.C. - 5th century A.D.) is the dawn of philosophy in the West. The first known philosopher in the West, Thales of Melitus (Melitus is an island off the west coast of Asia Minor), said everything is made of water. He was followed by other philosophers whom we group together as the *Presocrates*, philosophers who lived and worked before Socrates.

Socrates (470?-399 B.C.), who was put to death for not believing in the gods of the city-state of Athens, Greece and for corrupting the youth, remains one of the most important figures in philosophy. Although he left no written works of which we know, his process of teaching by asking questions (the dialectical *question and answer* method), his view that philosophy is a way of life and his martyrdom for philosophy have sealed his influence for all time. His student, Plato, who worked in every major area of philosophy, was the first great systematic philosopher in the West and remains influential today. He founded *The Academy* in Athens, which was, in effect, the first university in history.

Aristotle differed from Plato in some important respects. Unlike Plato, who was a rationalist, Aristotle was an empiricist. Philosophers today all tend to be either more Platonic or more Aristotelian. Aristotle founded *The Lyceum* in Athens, another school of philosophy. He and his followers were called *the peripatetics* (from *peri*, "around" and *pateo*, "to walk") due to Aristotle's habit of walking with his students while teaching.

After these major figures, a number of philosophical schools developed: *Stoicism*, *Epicureanism*, and later, *Neoplatonism*. Major changes also occurred in the Roman Empire near the end of the ancient period of philosophy. Rome first tolerated Christianity after a long period of off and on persecution, then made it the official religion of the Roman Empire. The Western part of the Roman Empire was decaying and would eventually fall to barbarian kings, a process that was formally completed at the largely symbolic date of 476 with the abdication of the last Western Roman Emperor, Romulus Augustulus. While the Empire lasted in the East until 1453, it did not focus on creative philosophy but on the preservation and transmission of Christian teaching.

The major Western transitional figure during this time was Augustine (354-430). After going through a period in which he believed in a good god and an evil god as a *Manichean,* he became a *Neoplatonist* and then a Christian. When he died, he was Bishop of Hippo in North Africa. He was a rationalist influenced heavily by Plato's followers, the Neoplatonists. He tried to combine Neoplatonism and Christianity, and he believed that faith and reason are complementary.

Medieval and Renaissance Philosophy

The medieval period in philosophy lasted from around 400-1400, with the Renaissance period following. Religious issues dominated philosophy in such notable figures as Anselm of Canterbury (1033-1109) and Thomas Aquinas. The latter was influenced by Aristotle, the Neoplatonists, the Jewish philosopher Moses Maimonides (1135-1204), and the Arab philosophers Averroes (1126-1198) and Avicenna (980?-1037) as well as by Augustine. Aquinas attempted to reconcile Aristotle's thought with Christianity. Both he and Anselm used a *scholastic method* to do philosophy. This method focused on careful argumentation with objections to a thesis listed, followed by the master's answer and replies to objections. Like Augustine, these philosophers believed that faith and reason are complementary rather than contradictory.

John Duns Scotus (1265?-1308) differed from Aquinas in important respects, but was in the same general tradition of reconciling faith and reason. He was a brilliant philosopher; however, some of his followers were not, and they were called *Dunses* - that is the source of the *dunce* cap.

William of Occam (1287-1347) began the separation of faith and reason that led to the secular world we see in Europe and the United States today. He denied that universal terms such as *humanity* refer to anything more than individuals. This eventually led to the view that since the natures to which universal terms supposedly refer are unreal, human beings can manipulate nature as they please, including human nature.

The Renaissance period (roughly 1300-1600) was a time of significant change in Europe. There was a renewed interest in Classical Greece and

Rome which was accelerated by the fall of the Eastern Roman (Byzantine) Empire in 1453, when complete manuscripts of Plato and other ancient writers made it to Western Europe. On October 31, 1517, Martin Luther (1483-1546) nailed his 95 Theses to the door of the church in Wittenberg, Germany, sparking the Protestant Reformation. With new classical sources available, there was a revival of Platonism and Neoplatonism. Cardinal Nicholas of Cusa (1401-1464) developed a near-pantheistic conception of God and nature with insights from Platonic and Neoplatonic thought. Yet with this revival of learning also came the rise of occult movements. Although most so-called *witches* who were executed during this period were innocent, witchcraft and magic did experience a revival during the Renaissance period, as did the practice of alchemy, which was more of a way of life than merely a means of turning base metals into gold. The end of this turbulent period led to the religious warfare of the seventeenth century, including the Thirty Years' War, a brutal conflict between Roman Catholics and Protestants that lasted from 1618-1648. In some areas of Europe, especially in Germany, a third of the population died. The Peace of Westphalia that ended the war is credited with creating the modern nation-state.

Modern Philosophy

Even during the period of mass bloodshed, modern science was rising with Galileo's defense of Copernicus' theory of a sun-centered solar system and other advances such as William Harvey's discovery of the circulation of blood. Unlike religious conflicts, which seemed to spark unending wars, scientific conflicts could be overcome through observation and experiment. It was the influence of the scientific revolution of the seventeenth century that sparked the era of modern philosophy.

Modern philosophy was optimistic, holding that if philosophy followed the method of science, it would make progress. Modern philosophers who were rationalist emphasized the mathematical side of science. These philosophers, including René Descartes, Benedict Spinoza (1632-1677) and Gottfried Leibniz (1646-1716), were called the *Continental Rationalists* since they worked on the continent of Europe outside of England. In England, however, philosophers from the time of Francis Bacon on focused on the experimental side of science and were thus empiricists. Three highly regarded *British Empiricists* were John Locke, George Berkeley (1685-1753) and David Hume.

Yet philosophy did not make progress. Continental rationalism produced three contradictory metaphysical systems. British empiricism ended in radical skepticism that seemed to deny any basis for the reliability of science. The greatest of the modern philosophers, Immanuel Kant, tried to clean up the mess by bringing aspects of rationalism and empiricism together (though Kant was primarily a rationalist). After Kant, philosophers reacted to his views in different ways and philosophy again was divided into different schools of thought. G. W. F. Hegel (1770-1831) was a metaphysician of the old school, developing a comprehensive system of reality based on the development of mind in human history. Almost everyone has heard of Karl Marx (1818-1883), the founder of modern Communism. At the end of the nineteenth century a prophetic figure, Friedrich Nietzsche (1844-1900), appeared, who saw through the hypocrisy of a secular Europe holding on to the remnants of Christianity. Yet he did not buy into the evolutionary optimism of the nineteenth century, holding that all events are repeated the same way over and over - an eternal return.

Contemporary Philosophy: "Schools" of Thought

The old optimism was destroyed in Europe by World War I (1914-1918) in which 20 million people were killed or died due to disease or deprivation of basic resources. Immediately after the war, a flu epidemic killed another 20 million people. World War I marked the end of the modern era in philosophy and the beginning of contemporary philosophy.

Analytic (Anglo-American) Philosophy

Contemporary philosophy is divided into two major categories. The first is *Analytic* (or Anglo-American) philosophy, which is prominent in the United States, the United Kingdom and some of the Scandinavian countries. Analytic philosophy tends to focus on logic and philosophical problems in language. Some analytic philosophers, such as Bertrand Russell, tried to develop an ideal language. Others, such as the later Ludwig Wittgenstein (1889-1951), focused on ordinary language. There was a subgroup of analytic philosophers called the *logical positivists* who believed that any statement that was not a tautology (for example, "A dog is a dog") or verifiable by the senses is meaningless. This position was attacked on the grounds that the above principle on which it is based is neither a tautology nor an empirically verifiable statement. In the last fifty years, analytic philosophy has broadened to the point that many philosophers in this school deal with traditional philosophical problems such as the existence of God, but with great attention to logic, especially modern symbolic logic.

Continental Philosophy
(Phenomenology, Existentialism, and Postmodernism)

Continental philosophy consists of *phenomenology* and *existentialism*, as well as *postmodernism*. It is practiced primarily in continental Europe, especially in France and Germany. Phenomenology was actually invented by an American, Charles Sanders Peirce (1839-1914), but his work remained relatively unknown until recently. In Europe, Edmund Husserl (1859-1938), is considered the inventor of the phenomenological method. This method involves suspending any presuppositions about reality when examining an experience and describing, in a disciplined way, the experience as a whole so that nothing important is missed. If I am walking in a moonlit field at night, I can describe the experience as a whole - I am not concerned about the reality of moonlight or what causes the moon - my focus is on how that entire experience is affecting me. Literature is a good way to describe such experiences, so it is no surprise that many phenomenologists write literary works.

The phenomenological method works well for existentialist philosophers, who focus on the concrete individual existing in the world, not on abstract human nature. There are two major kinds of existentialists: *atheistic* and *theistic*. Atheistic existentialists, as the name suggests, do not believe in God. They focus on people as thrown into a world in which they did not ask to be born (the line in "Riders on the Storm" by The Doors, "into this world we're thrown" captures this concept exactly). "Thrown-ness" (*Geworfenheit* in German) is a term used by a philosopher, Martin Heidegger (1889-1976), who is often grouped with the existentialists, but denied he was one. Other famous atheistic existentialists are Jean-Paul Sartre (1905-1980) and Albert Camus (1913-1960). They denied there is a set human nature, so human beings must make themselves by making choices and being responsible for those choices. The 1960s imperative, "Do your own thing," is existentialist in tone.

Theistic existentialists believe in God. They include a philosopher ahead of his time, Søren Kierkegaard (1813-1855), as well as Gabriel Marcel (1889-1973), Karl Jaspers (1883-1969) and Martin Buber (1878-1965). They focus on God as the source of meaning in what otherwise would be a meaningless universe.

In recent years, Continental philosophy has focused on how so much of what humans call knowledge seems specific to cultures. Michel Foucault (1926-1984), although not a total relativist, believed that as society changes, patterns of thinking in the sciences and other disciplines change as well. This does not mean that all is relative -Foucault tended to accept modern science as a fairly reliable source of knowledge - only that knowledge is not independent of history and culture. Jacques Derrida (1930-2004) was far more radical, denying there is any objective meaning in texts - he believed that the only meaning in a text is the meaning the reader provides.

Of course there are other schools and subgroups in philosophy - Marxists, Thomists (followers of the thought of Thomas Aquinas), Process Philosophers, Feminist Philosophers, and many more. As long as humans exist on this planet, philosophical questions will arise and philosophical debates will take place.

How to Use this Book

Philosophy is both a theoretical and practical discipline involving hard intellectual work. The exercises in this book encourage you to engage in philosophical reasoning through the dialectical, or Socratic method. Socrates used a question and answer method in doing philosophy - that is, he would ask a question, listen to the response, critique it, and ask another question. These exercises ask you to engage in a specific task - you will get the most out of the exercises if you actually perform the task, though you can imagine performing it, too. There are questions throughout each exercise that encourage you to think about the activity. Each exercise mentions philosophers' and other thinkers' ideas on an issue relating to that particular exercise. Most often, I have chosen people who disagree with one another so you can see arguments for both sides of an issue. Discover your own answer to the questions in each exercise and consider how you justify the answer using reason and experience. You may find some inconsistencies in your answers to various questions - in that case, you need to re-examine your position to see if you can reconcile the inconsistencies. Contradictions cannot be true, so you will have to rethink your positions in such a way that the contradiction disappears. You may find that after you work through several exercises that you change your mind about your answer to a previous exercise. This is a good thing, since it shows you are thinking. I hope you have fun with these exercises and discover the deep joy that arises from actually doing philosophy.

METAPHYSICS

LOOK AT A PHOTO OF YOURSELF AS A CHILD

Are you sitting on a white plastic swing seat, grinning for the camera? Are you scowling, standing in front of your aunts and uncles and your mom just *had* to take a picture? Perhaps you are celebrating your first communion or your Bar or Bat Mitzvah. Look at your face in the photo - is that face really yours? But you have changed so much - you are taller, heavier, your hair is different, you wear a different style of clothing. Your mind has changed, too. You're more mature and have learned so much about life and about the world. Maybe you are more religious than when you were younger, or perhaps your faith has been drifting away over the years, falling like maple leaves after the first frost. You may have changed career plans, moving from a childhood dream of being the first astronaut on Mars to your present plans for a career in accounting, computer graphic design, or law.

You stare at the photo and what do you see? How do you feel? Startled? Scared? Does your childhood seem as distant as relatives who rarely visit? Or is there a great deal of continuity between you in the photo and you today? Perhaps you still have the same quirky smile or quick temper, the same love of football, sports cars, figure skating or gymnastics. You come to believe that the child in the photo is closer to you than a twin - you recognize that the photograph represents you as you were then.

The issue of what makes you the same person over time has haunted philosophers since ancient times. Some philosophers, such as David Hume, Derek Parfit (1942-), and The Buddha (6th century B.C.) believe that you are *not* the same person over time, because there is no such thing as personal identity - *there is no you.* Such thinkers deny the existence of any permanent *self* or *soul.* To them, your childhood face in the photo represents a different person or *person stage* than the person you are today. Your memories from childhood are like thoughts about a distant relative, although your memories of your "self" five minutes ago are more like memories of a very close relative, a near twin.

Other philosophers believe that you have a stable personal identity over time. Plato thought that having the same *soul* makes you the same person today as you were when you were a child. Similarly, René

Descartes held that you are a *thinking thing* and that having the same *consciousness* over time makes you the same person throughout your lifetime. John Locke modified this view. For Locke, if you have a stream of memories going back in time, then that is evidence that you are the same person today as you were in the past. If your memories stretch back to the time in your life of your childhood photo, you are the same person as that child. For these thinkers, it is your *mind* or *soul* that makes you who you are, not your physical body. Even if you had magically changed bodies so that the body in the photo is not your present body, you are still the same person as the child in the photo as long as you have the same mind or soul.

A middle of the road position is that of Aristotle and St. Thomas Aquinas, who believed that your identity depends on your having the same body-soul *composite* over time. That is, it is your body and soul *together* that make you *you*. According to this position, you are the same person as the child in the photo because you have the same body and soul now as you had as a child.

So now ask yourself again, "Who *is* that person in the photo?"

REFLECTIONS ON A RAINY DAY

Outside, it is raining so hard you would think the clouds were crying. Maybe you have plans for today: playing basketball, relaxing with a round of golf, playing tennis with a friend, shopping at a flea market. But you are stuck inside your apartment or dorm room, frustrated by your lack of freedom, bound by nature's necessity.

But are you really bound by necessity? Can't you leave at any time? Why can't you shoot some solo hoops on the outdoor court? Assuming there is no lightning, there is little danger other than slipping, and you have heard that catching colds from getting wet is a myth. You *can* go out if you wish. You have *chosen* to stay inside, *chosen* to allow circumstances to dictate your actions - in which case these circumstances seem less dictatorial, right?

Suppose that you hate getting wet; you find soggy, matted hair uncomfortable. Okay, so it *is* your choice to stay inside, but you are still miserable because of the change in your plans. Why allow what has happened to affect you so much? You cannot control the weather, but as the ancient Stoic philosophers noted, you *can* control your *reaction* to the weather. You may have a sense that this was the way things were meant to be, that nature or God has ordered things this way and the best thing you can do is to accept the rain with serenity, feeling calm, peaceful and free from care.

So on this rainy day you have a choice. If there is no thunder and lightning, you may choose outside activities. You may decide to stick to your original plan, as much as you can given the circumstances, and play basketball with the ball slapping the water on the concrete. Tell your friends the game is still on. Who knows? Some of them may show up.

On the other hand, you might decide to alter your outdoor plans: you open your door and dance in the rain, or walk in the woods and watch raindrops drip through leaves onto the soggy path. If you are concerned about getting wet, wear a raincoat and waterproof boots, and carry an umbrella.

You may decide to stay indoors, take a nap, read a good book, listen to music and invite your friends for food and games. You decide - but then ask yourself what that means. Perhaps you will discover that you have the free will to choose and change your circumstances. Perhaps you become more convinced than ever that you are determined by outside circumstances. You may find free will empowering, for you recognize that you can change your seemingly negative circumstances - or you may find freedom disconcerting, for you feel naked and alone, without purpose or plan.

Outside my window it is raining too. And so, perhaps we make this choice together, or at least together we can find solace in our shared circumstances.

LISTEN TO YOUR HEARTBEAT

I s your life something you take for granted, something that seems to escape time? When you go about your daily tasks: studying, talking with friends, going to the beach, partying, do you normally say to yourself, "I'm alive and studying," or "I'm alive and partying with friends"? Perhaps not, since your life is something presupposed in whatever you do, for otherwise there would be no *you* to do anything!

Most of us feel that we are immortal, that death's skeletal arm will never snatch us away into nothingness. At an intellectual level we know the truth of the syllogism, "All human beings are mortal; Socrates is a human being; therefore Socrates is mortal," but that is an abstract concept that will not affect us personally. Even our experience is not sufficient for us to destroy belief in our immortality. Although we experience time and change, the movement of the seasons, the life and death of our pets, witness the funerals of friends and relatives - and our own body changing with age - we believe that we will be immune from death. The existence of other people may be contingent - but *our own* existence is necessary. The common lot of humanity will exempt *us*. Other human beings just aren't as lucky.

Have you ever listened to your heartbeat? If not, borrow a stethoscope from a friend or purchase an inexpensive model. Place it over your heart and listen. Do you hear (I hope!) a strong and regular beat? You feel as if you are hearing your very life pulsing with each *lub-dup*. Nothing seems more strong and sure, nothing seems more faithful, than the steady beat of your heart. Imagine listening to it a year from now, ten years from now, twenty - even if you have a few wrinkles on your face, even if your body moves more slowly than before, your heart will have the same healthy sound. It will last forever - and so will you.

Think of each heartbeat as a moment in time. Once that moment in time is lost, it has perished, passed out of existence forever. *Lub-dup* - a moment dies. *Lub-dup, lub dup*... and moments roll by so quickly that you lose count. Alfred North Whitehead said that each moment is "perpetually perishing." For Whitehead, this was not a bad thing, since new, creative moments arise from the ashes of the old. But you may not feel so comforted, for you sense moments slipping away like a balloon sliding from a child's hand - the balloon is lost, never to be regained.

Yet this can be a positive thing, for discomfort can drive a person to think. So let us think through this exercise and its implications. Each moment in time is perpetually perishing. You have used each beat of your heart to mark these dying moments. Every one of your heartbeats is a nonrepeatable event, passing away forever in a second or less. You may begin to realize that your own life is finite, limited in time. Your life passes away just as each one of your heartbeats passes away. Like rocks, trees and stars, you are contingent - it is possible for you *not* to exist. You *can* die, pass out of existence at any time. You know this from experience, for you know that other people have died, perhaps some of your loved ones. Unlike the contingency of a rock, this contingency *matters* to you in the most intimate way. The truth may appear to approach you too fast - that *you* are contingent, that *you* will one day pass out of existence, that *you* have only a finite number of heartbeats. Each one eats away at your life, just like the mice in a Tolstoy tale found in his book, *My Confession*, which are nibbling at the rope to which a man clings for his life, dangling over a well. At the bottom of the well is a dragon that represents death.

When you listen to your heart, do its beats sound out the wonder of your existence, the joy that you are alive and aware, or do they warn of your impending death? Could it be both? Martin Heidegger said that we are in a state of *being towards death*, a condition that both makes us anxious and drives us to action, since we realize that our lives are finite and there is only so much time to accomplish things. Is our finitude the source of our success? Or is it frightening, the *one-less* of each heartbeat a harbinger of future nothingness?

Remove the stethoscope from your chest, take the ear pieces out of your ears. Listen to other sounds: birds singing as they build their nests, cars turning into drives as the workday ends or fellow students walking down your dorm hall after returning from class. Have things that seemed so obvious, things you took for granted - your own life - increased almost infinitely in value? Is it a good day to be alive?

PHOTOGRAPH A REFLECTION IN WATER

Visit a lake, a slowly flowing river or a creek. Find a calm spot where the water is an unrippled mirror reflecting the trees overhanging the bank. Aim a camera at the water, taking care to photograph only the pool and its reflections. After the film is developed, take the photo and turn it so that the trees are right-side-up. Now examine the photo. Pretend you are seeing it for the first time, that it is, perhaps, an old photo found in a box in the attic.

What do you see? Trees, for sure. Do they look real? Can you tell, since you've "never seen" this photo before, that you are looking at a reflection? Would it matter to you whether the photo is of a reflection or of the actual trees? Isn't the photo itself only an image of the trees and not the trees themselves? Yet if the photo is of a reflection of the trees, isn't it just an image of an image, a copy of a copy? Is a copy as good as the real thing?

In Plato's *Allegory of the Cave,* several people have been chained all their lives to posts in a cave. They are facing the back wall of the cave. Behind them is a flickering fire that causes shadows to dance on the wall. Between the fire and the prisoners is a place where individuals play with puppets, causing particular kinds of shadows; for example, a puppet of a dog would cause a dog-shaped shadow to appear on the wall. Since the world of shadows is the only world the prisoners have known, they take the shadows to be what is real.

One day, someone decides to untie a prisoner and turn him around toward the fire. Of course he is blinded by the light and will have the same near-blind experience when he is led outside the cave. Slowly he adjusts to his new surroundings, moving from observing shadows of trees and reflections in water to viewing the things-in-themselves - finally (at least in Plato's account!), he will be able to look on the sun, the source of all light, directly.

For Plato, most of us are the prisoners in the cave, for we believe that the world of our senses is ultimately real. Plato believed that trees, dogs, cats, buildings and human bodies are mere shadows, not the highest reality. It is the world of the Forms which is ultimately real - Forms are not in space, not in time, but they make everything else possible, including our experience of this world of shadows. Since the world of our sense experience is constantly changing, it gives us neither stability nor firm truth. The world of the Forms, however, never changes. When we say something true about a Form, it is always true.

The individual dog we see on this earth *participates* (in some way which Plato does not clarify) in the Form of Dogness which really exists in this *higher* world with other Forms. There are also Forms of *Catness*, *Humanity*, as well as Forms of *Numbers* and *Truth* and *Beauty*. The objects outside the cave represent the Forms, and the sun represents the highest Form, the Form of the Good. The dogs and cats and trees we see around us are, in some sense, imperfect copies of the Forms of *Dogness*, *Catness* and *Treeness*. If we believe the trees we see with our eyes are ultimately real, we fail to recognize that they are illusory, shadows on the wall of the cave. Even lower on the scale of reality are works of art - a painting of a tree, for example, is a copy of a tree from the world of our senses, which in turn is a copy of the Form of *Treeness*. It is merely a copy of a copy. Plato was not fond of artists, for they are peddlers in double illusion.

Look at the photo again. Examine every detail in it, every tree, every branch, every leaf. Isn't the photo a reflection of trees - doesn't that mean that it is a copy of a copy? Is the photo less real than the reflection in water? Is the reflection less real than the trees? What if you notice details in the photo that you would not notice otherwise? Would this change your opinion? What about the reflection - is it less beautiful than the trees because it is a copy, or does it add its own beauty to the world? Does the photograph add any beauty or goodness to the world, or is it a mere copy, a shadow on a cave's wall? Does it, perhaps, preserve the changing beauty of nature in a form that seems, for the moment, without change?

RUN OVER A MIRAGE

You are driving on a straight stretch of highway on a hot summer day. The sun is so bright the glare almost blinds you. Even with the air conditioner on full-force, you feel warm and wish rain would pour down to cool the outside air. On a straight stretch of road you see a silver pool in the distance. You believe it is water and slow down, though you are not sure whether the "pool" is really water or a mirage. In any case, you drive and run over - what? The "water" seems to disappear beneath your tires, with more "water" forming in front of you as you continue to drive. Most likely you will conclude that what you're running over is not water. But why? What is different about the behavior of this pool from the usual behavior of water?

What is it that makes water *water*? Some philosophers, such as Aristotle, believed that natural objects have *natures*. A nature is something which makes an entity what it is. For example, the nature of table salt makes it the kind of thing it is, a compound with the chemical formula NaCl (since it is composed of sodium and chlorine, chemists call table salt "Sodium Chloride") and accounts for it behaving in characteristic ways (such as being involved in chemical reactions in our cells which are necessary for us to live). Aristotle's approach would determine what something is by how it behaves and what kind of changes it causes in other things.

Do you notice that water, wherever it may be found, behaves in characteristic ways? Water is liquid at room temperature. Our bodies are made of mostly water, and we drink it for survival. If you are driving through water, you can hear it splash when your tires hit a puddle. It normally does not disappear as you approach it, then reform in the distance.

Could there be a situation in which water does not behave in the usual way? If the pool disappears in front of your car, how can you know that the pool is not actually filled with water? Do you think this is possible? Or do you think that water will always behave in a stable way, so if something does not *behave* like water, it is no longer water?

Perhaps you conclude that what you are viewing is a mirage, an illusion. You may have heard a scientific explanation of what appears to be water, that the silver sheen on the highway, is a reflection of the sky. Appearance diverges from reality; what looks like water turns out to be something else entirely.

Yet even if the pool is an illusion, it has some reality. After all, you see *something* in the road. When we talk of *illusions* and *mirages*, do we refer to total non-entities? Doesn't a mirage or illusion exist in some sense? Then how? One answer could be that the mirage really exists as a reflection, but does *not* exist as a pool of water. In that case the issue becomes a matter of accurately identifying the pool.

Suppose you live in a culture which has not yet encountered modern science, a culture whose view of the world is supported by myth. You are tired and thirsty as you search for an oasis in the desert. Ahead, you spot what appears to be water, but when you reach the site, it fades away, and more forms in the distance. How might you interpret the disappearing *water*? Is it a trick of some devious deity, who withdraws water just as it comes within your reach? Or did a demon create an illusion of water which is really only shadow? Do you think that if you were in such a culture you would ask the same questions about the experience as you would in this culture? Is there a reality over and above mere appearance, a reality that is stable despite illusions, stable no matter what culture in which you live?

Keep driving through the pools. Perhaps one day you will be surprised by the sound of a splash.

TRY TO CROSS THE FINISH LINE

Find a spot to mark out a straight path on which to walk. It may be part of an athletic track or in your back yard - any place where you can freely walk. Measure out twenty paces. Make marks in the dirt or place something on the ground to identify your starting and finish lines. Ideally you should be able to see where you have marked the finish when you are standing at the starting line.

Step up to the starting line and notice the finish line a short distance ahead. You might think it an easy task to get from point A to point B; all you have to do is walk a few seconds and you are there. Walk ten paces and stop. You are half way to the end. Now walk five more paces and stop. You are now at another halfway point, three-fourths of the way toward your goal. Walk two and a half paces. You are at another halfway point. Keep doing this, walking halfway, carefully measuring out your paces. Your shoes may get so close to the line that it will be physically impossible for you to measure another halfway point. It may appear that the tips of your shoes have reached the finish line and you should congratulate yourself. You might start to wonder about the point of this exercise.

If you think about mathematics and the nature of a straight line, you might conclude that you can never reach the finish line, since no matter how many halfway points you pass, there is always another halfway point. There are an infinite number of points in your tiny track, and you cannot pass through them all using a finite number of steps.

So you are stuck, right? It seems impossible to walk from one point to another. Is that movement really just an illusion? Parmenides (5th century B.C.) thought so. He sharply distinguished between what is real and what appears to be real. He believed that change does not occur and that the universe is a sphere, godlike and motionless. Parmenides went even further, holding that the universe is not only unchanging, but an indivisible whole. Although our everyday experience tells us that there are many things - other people, cats, trees, rocks, stars - they are not real.

Parmenides' student, Zeno of Elia (5th century B.C.), agreed, and his *paradoxes* are attempts to prove Parmenides' point that all motion is an illusion. You may be familiar with some of these, such as the paradox of the Tortoise and the Hare. The tortoise and hare are about to begin a race, with the tortoise given a slight head start. Although it appears that the hare is a much faster runner and should easily win the race, there is a problem. Since the hare must get halfway to the tortoise's present location, by then, the tortoise will have moved a little further. Then the hare has to get halfway to the tortoise's new location, ad infinitum - and the hare will never catch up. Thus, the motion of both tortoise and hare must be an illusion.

This exercise is based on another of Zeno's paradoxes. He believed it is impossible to move any distance, because to get from your starting point to the end you would have to cross an infinite number of points. Are you convinced by Parmenides and Zeno? Is motion an illusion? Is it really impossible for you to cross a finish line? Go back to the starting line again and begin walking until you have passed the finish line. Your senses tell you that you did precisely what Zeno said you could not do. However, Zeno would reply that your senses are unreliable and cannot reveal reality, but only appearances. Knowledge of reality comes through reason alone - and reason tells you that you cannot walk from one point to another. Could he be right? Are there any reasonable alternatives to Zeno's arguments? If reason contradicts sense experience, should you follow reason or sense experience? How does your view of reality, of what the world is really like, influence how you think you gain knowledge of the world? How does your view of how you gain knowledge of the world affect your view of reality? Do your answers to the previous two questions affect your reaction to the positions of Parmenides and Zeno?

Return to the starting line and sprint as fast as you can across the finish line. Do you now have the power to cross an infinite number of points? Maybe Parmenides was wrong: it is not the universe that is godlike, but you. Or is it possible that sense experience is more accurate than he and Zeno thought; the problem is not with *reason* itself, but with Zeno's *reasoning* in his paradoxes. Can the paradox be resolved?

IMAGINE SLEEP AS DEATH

I magine a day in which you are dead tired. The only thing to which you look forward is a good night's sleep. You crawl into bed and sleep soundly. When you wake up after such a night, do you ever feel as if there has been no passage of time between your going to bed and awakening? Do you ever wake up in such situations without remembering dreaming? Although you may have forgotten dreams you experienced, practically the result is that you feel as if you have never dreamed.

One morning when you wake up after a deep sleep, ask yourself, "Is a dreamless sleep different from death?" Suspend for a moment any belief you have in a life after death that involves conscious experience. Suppose death to be the annihilation of all personality and consciousness. This is how the followers of the Greek philosopher Epicurus (341-270 B.C.) understood death. If death is absolute unconsciousness, and dreamless sleep is also the annihilation of consciousness, is this sleep temporary death? Is it possible for death to be temporary? We have heard of people (and perhaps you know some of them) whose hearts have stopped beating and were resuscitated. Were they temporarily dead? Or is death an absolute boundary from which you cannot return?

Plato wrote the *Apology* about his teacher Socrates, who was on trial for not believing in the gods of Athens and for corrupting the youth. Eventually Socrates was convicted and sentenced to death. In his speech after the penalty phase of the trial, Socrates sought to reassure his friends that death is not something evil. He argued that death is either absolute nothingness or the soul living on after death. Let us consider the second possibility - that the soul lives on after death. Socrates believes that this would be wonderful, for he would enjoy engaging in philosophical conversations with the heroes of old such as Achilles. Do you think you would enjoy existence after death as a disembodied soul? Can a disembodied soul experience anything?

The first possibility relates more to the notion of sleep as death. Socrates says if death is nothingness, then it is no different from a dreamless sleep. Don't you feel refreshed after a dreamless sleep? Death is one eternal night's sleep. What can be better than that? Do you agree with Socrates?

Another philosopher who compares sleep to death is David Hume. Hume believes that death is the obliteration of all consciousness. He asks whether a dreamless sleep is really the same as death and answers his own question: "Yes." Since a person is unconscious in dreamless sleep, such sleep is a temporary death.

Whether or not you agree with Hume, imagine that he (and Socrates) are right and that sleep really is equivalent to death. You wake up one morning and realize that you have just come back to life. Is the knowledge that you were temporarily dead disconcerting? Do you feel that you literally passed out of existence during sleep? If so, then how can it make sense for something to constantly come to be and pass away? Are there any implications for the medical determination of death? If you are really dead when you are asleep, then if you became permanently unconscious, even if you were still breathing, would you be permanently dead? If you do not believe you are dead when you are sleeping, what do you believe?

Supposing Hume is right, would your disappearance during sleep make you anxious about the time you will die for good? Would your permanent disappearance be good, bad or neutral? Does the prospect of permanently losing consciousness frighten you? If not, why? If so, is fear or some other emotion - or no emotion at all - the appropriate response to death?

When you go to bed tonight, will you sleep any easier? Or will it be more difficult as you consider whether you will soon disappear?

REBUILD A HOUSE WITH BLOCKS

Find or buy a set of children's building blocks, preferably plastic pieces that snap together. Choose blocks of the same size and color; use them to build a house (*House 1*). Take the house apart, block by block, carefully noting where each block was located in House 1. Using the same blocks, rebuild the house, placing each block in the exact location it had in House 1. There now exists *House 2*. Tear this house down, this time, not keeping up with where you placed each block. Shuffle the blocks around in a pile. Then rebuild the house in exactly the same shape as it was before (*House 3*). Take the house apart again. Choose a different set of blocks, but of the same size and color as the original blocks. Now build the house, still using the same pattern as you used before (*House 4*).

Are any of the houses you built after the original house the *same house* as House 1? What about House 2? Does taking the house apart destroy its identity? Does it regain its identity when you build House 2? Yet how can something lose its identity and then get it back? That seems as if something disappears and then comes back into existence. If the identity of House 1 is not destroyed, then how does it keep its identity when it is just a pile of blocks on your living room floor?

Is House 3 the same house as House 1? It is built of the same blocks, looks the same as the first house, only the blocks are in different locations than they were before. Does this make a difference for the identity of the house? Do the blocks have to be in *exactly* the same location as in House 1 for the identity of the house to be preserved? Then what about House 4, in which you used a wholly different set of blocks? Does the fact that they look the same and are of the same color as the other blocks matter? Does the fact that all the houses are built according to exactly the same pattern make a difference for identity?

What if, instead of totally tearing down House 1, you replace one block with another? Is it the same house as it was before? What if you replace two blocks? Half of the blocks? What if the replacement blocks are of a different color or size than the originals? What if you do not change the original blocks, but add an addition to the house, such as an extra room or a porch?

Identity - that which makes an object the same object over time - is a tough issue. Philosophers have argued back and forth for ages about the correct criteria for identity. Some believe that having the same pattern over time makes something the same entity. Aristotle held such a view. He believed that having the same form accounts for identity. However, he was primarily thinking of biological organisms - a dog is the same dog over time because it has the same form or pattern over time, even though its matter changes through eating, assimilation of nutrients and elimination. Would the same principle also apply to inanimate objects, such as a house? Take the example of the block houses. Once you build a block house according to a specific pattern, does it remains the same house even if a few blocks are replaced over time?

David Hume did not believe in a literal identity over time, either for living things or inanimate objects. He believed that it is necessary for an object to be unchanging over time to retain its identity - but objects are constantly changing. Some changes may be invisible. For example, your bed looks the same from morning to morning when you get up, but the matter out of which the bed is constructed has slightly changed: molecules have moved, fuzz from the sheets has sloughed off, small flecks of paint have fallen from the frame. You can *call* it the same bed because your mind remembers that the bed today is similar in appearance to the bed yesterday, but strictly speaking (according to Hume), it's *not* the same bed. But is it? Let us return to the house examples. According to Hume, does House 1 retain its identity from moment to moment? How does the answer effect one's position on the identities of Houses 2, 3 and 4?

Does anything keep its identity over time? If so, how? If not, how do you feel about a world that seems to have no stability? Since your cells in your body are constantly changing, what becomes of your own identity?

REARRANGE YOUR ROOM

Rearrange your room, but do it in such a way you hate the result. Move your desk and other pieces of furniture to different places, places you would prefer them not to be. Move your computer to the other side of your desk. Rearrange the books in your bookcase so it is more difficult to locate a title. Move any posters on your wall to different locations. Choose one poster you like, remove it and replace it with a different one that you do not like.

Are you comfortable with the changes or do you feel out of place? Leave your room for an hour, shutting the door behind you. When you return and open your door, what is your reaction? Are the changes cosmetic, nothing more than your room looking differently than before, or is there something more to them than the fact that you dislike them? Do you believe that you have changed because your room has changed? If so, have you changed for the worse or for the better? Do you think you will grow to like the changes over time?

How much of what makes you a unique individual goes into the way you arrange your room? Is it possible that your room and the objects in it are an extension of yourself? On the other hand, is it the case that your room is just a place for you to sleep at night and store things, perhaps work on your computer - with no more value than its usefulness? Could it be replaced by other rooms of different styles and arrangements without making any difference to you? Maybe it has no unique nature of its own.

This view might be false, however. Is it possible that your room has an individual nature that you have created by arranging it in your own unique way? Could it be more like your individual work of art rather than a place to sleep and work? John Duns Scotus was one of the first philosophers to focus on the individual thing, such as a particular flower or human being. He believed that a human being has a human nature as well as an animal nature. But an individual human being reveals what it is to be human and animal in a unique way. Duns Scotus believed there had to be something to account for the individuality of a particular human being (and of a particular tree, cow, cat, etc.). This *something* he called *haecceitas*, literally *thisness*. It is *thisness* that makes something the unique thing it is. We cannot know something's (or someone's) *haecceitas* directly. But we might know it indirectly, for example, by seeing hints of it in the beauty of a particular rose or in the actions of a particular human being.

If what makes you the individual you are is your *haecceitas*, is it possible that some of that rubs off when you arrange your room? If you feel disconcerted or lost when you arrange your room in a style you dislike, could this be a form of identity crisis? When you rearrange your room, does it lose the *thisness* you gave it, an individual uniqueness which somehow reflects your own unique individuality?

Thomas Aquinas believed something made reflects its maker's character in a special way. For example, part of a painter's wisdom and character can be discovered through that individual's paintings. Is your room like a painting? Could someone understand a bit of who you are by examining your room?

What about your rearrangement? Were you really able to arrange things totally differently than before, or do you find that certain patterns remain the same? What if, when you get used to the new shape of the room, you like it better than the original? What has changed: you, the room, or both?

TALK TO YOUR PET

If you have a pet, whether it be a dog, cat, bird or snake, set aside some time to talk to it. Pick any topic of conversation you like - from politics to video games to the best dog or cat food. Look your pet in the eye. Do you notice any sign that your pet understands what you are saying? Try some variations, such as giving your pet a command. If your dog sits when you say "Sit!" do you think the dog understands the word "sit"? If your lizard seems more active when you are praising how beautiful it is, does it understand your words as praise?

The ability of non-human animals to think has long been debated in the history of philosophy. A few philosophers, such as René Descartes, held that non-human animals neither feel nor think, but are mere machines. It is obvious that Descartes also denied that animals understand language. A more moderate position is represented by Aristotle. He believed that non-human animals have a life principle, a *soul*, but not a rational soul like human beings. According to Aristotle, such animals have a *sensitive soul*, which gives them the ability to feel emotions. Some higher animals, such as mammals, have the ability to make primitive judgments concerning, for example, hunting prey. But since animals lack reason, they lack the ability to use and understand language. Your dog or cat may respond to your tone of voice and know when you're pleased, upset or ready to put food in the dish but cannot understand your words.

Do you think Aristotle is right? Have you ever had an experience which suggested your pet understands the meaning of words? Does your cat run away when you say to a friend, "I'm going to clip her claws?" Does your dog hide when you say the word "vet"? If your pets react this way, could there be another explanation for their behavior than their understanding your words? Could you tone of voice and body movements give clues to your pet so that she recognizes what is going to happen?

Must an animal be capable of speaking before it can understand language? Chimpanzees can make over thirty different sounds, but they are not able to form words due to the structure of their bodies. Could the sounds that chimpanzees and other animals make be a form of language?

33

Attempts have been made to teach some chimpanzees American Sign Language. Although some people believe that such experiments show that chimpanzees can understand and form words through sign language, others dispute this. Suppose there could be a way to teach a dog to make certain signs representing letters, perhaps by shaking a paw a certain number of times. If the dog seemed to form words and carry on a conversation, would this mean that it understands language? The same argument has been used against studies on African Grey Parrots, who can talk clearly, that seem to show them carrying on a conversation with a human being. If some animals understand sign language and others can speak a human language and understand some words in that language, would this have implications for the relationship between language and speech?

Is it possible that your pet's response to your words is due to conditioning? Suppose your cat runs under the bed if you say, "vet". Is it possible that the cat hears the sound of the word, "vet" without knowing its meaning? It may know that when you make such a sound, something unpleasant will follow - being picked up and put in its carrier, brought to a place where it knows it will feel a painful prick in its side. This might also be the case when an animal comes when you say, "It's time for supper." In addition, when you have a *conversation* with your pet using a pleasant tone of voice, your pet might find that comforting no matter what words you say.

If you know a second language other than English speak to your pet in that language. Does your pet respond differently? Try using English words in sentences that do not make sense. How does your pet respond? And if you do not feel too silly doing this, meow to your cat, bark to your dog or whistle to your bird (with a lizard or snake you are out of luck) and watch your pet's reaction.

COMPARE TOMATOES

Buy a tomato you pick from a shelf of your local grocery store. Then find a home grown tomato. If you or someone you know has a vegetable garden with tomatoes, pick one. Otherwise, buy your second tomato from a farmers' market. Take your two tomatoes home and slice them up. Eat a slice from one tomato, then the other. Keep doing this until you have finished both tomatoes. Do you notice any difference in the flavor? Does one tomato taste better than the other? Which one? If one does taste better, why?

Some people believe that home grown tomatoes taste better than store bought ones. They often claim that the store bought tomato has an *artificial* taste and that the home grown tomato tastes good because it is more *natural*. Sometimes they say the store bought tomato tastes "fake," as if somehow it were not a real tomato. If you liked the home grown tomato better, do you agree with these people's reasons for saying it is better? Is it true that some tomatoes are more *natural* than others? Suppose the store bought tomato was grown in a hydroponic solution (that is, grown in a container of water with nutrients dissolved in it, rather than being grown in soil). Would this tomato be more *artificial* than other tomatoes? What if it were true that the home grown tomato is somehow *more natural* than the store bought one? Would this imply that it is a better tomato or that it must necessarily taste better? Should we identify *good* with what is *natural*?

Is the alleged distinction between the *natural* and the *artificial* a valid one? Aristotle believed so. He thought a natural object, such as a horse or human being, is composed of form and matter. The form is what makes a horse a horse or a human being a human being. Matter can be considered a kind of wax tablet upon which forms are stamped. Form and matter cannot be separated, although matter may take on different forms (as when a horse dies and the form of the horse is replaced by the forms of the chemical elements that make up its body). The form of the horse includes all the elements essential to being a horse, such as its DNA structure, the fact that it is an herbivore, and so forth. Natural forms are found in objects that are not manufactured by human beings, such as the animals mentioned above, but also plants such as tomatoes, minerals such as quartz and elements such as hydrogen.

Artificial forms are different - they are imposed on matter by a human being. For example, the homebuilder imposes a particular form on the house based on the plans the architect drew up. Forms of houses, statues, computers, automobiles and other human-made objects are artificial forms. Where do your tomatoes fit in? Assume for the moment that Aristotle's position is right and see where it leads you. Is a tomato a *natural* or *artificial* product? The tomato varieties of the nineteenth century were much smaller than those today. Through selective breeding, larger varieties appeared. Does that mean that tomatoes today are artificial? Many home gardeners put chemical fertilizers on their plants. Would their tomatoes be more artificial than those grown by gardeners who use only cow manure for fertilizer? Would it make a difference if a tomato has been genetically altered by scientists?

Do you believe that the distinction between *natural* and *artificial* is a reasonable one? Or does the distinction work only regarding plants and animals that are not cultivated by human beings that live in the wild, in which case the only *natural* plants are the *wild* ones? Or perhaps tomatoes and other cultivated plants are a hybrid of *natural* and *artificial*, since they are manipulated by human beings. Another possibility is that *natural* and *artificial* are not absolutely distinct, but are on a continuum. Applied to tomatoes, it could be the case that a *home grown* tomato is eighty percent *natural*, while a *store bought* tomato is only fifty percent *natural*.

Does any of this really matter? Assuming both tomatoes are good for you and any human alterations have not introduced toxins into the tomato, is it really important whether a tomato is *natural* or *artificial* other than as a matter of taste?

EXAMINE A NATURAL OBJECT AND AN ARTIFICIAL COPY

Can something be more *real* than something else? Can *reality* have levels? What about *truth*? Can an object out there in the world be *truer* than another object? Or are sentences in a language the only thing that can be true or false?

Find a natural object. You can use your pet if you own one. If not, a flower or potted plant will do. Otherwise, find an apple or an orange.

Next, find an artificial copy of the natural object. If you own a beagle, then find a glass beagle or stuffed beagle at a store. If you have a potted plant, find a plastic plant, ideally of the same kind as your potted plant. If you have an apple or orange, find one of the fruit baskets with artificial fruit sold in hobby stores. Place the natural and artificial object side by side. Does it make sense to say that the natural object is *more real* than the artificial object? Suppose you put a natural apple next to a plastic apple. Is it true that the natural apple is a *real* apple and the plastic apple is not? Is the natural apple *more truly* an apple than the plastic one?

St. Thomas Aquinas believed in levels of reality, that some beings are *more real* than others. He thought the universe was a hierarchy of beings, from the lowliest (to modernize his language) quark to the highest and truest reality, God. In Aquinas' universe, it makes perfect sense to say that something is *more real* or *more true* than something else. Aquinas would have no problem saying that a natural apple is *more real* or *truer* than an artificial apple. Is Aquinas' correct? Even if you do not believe he is correct, does his position make better sense given your exercise using the natural and artificial objects?

Willard V. O. Quine, who taught philosophy many years at Harvard University, does not accept the notion of degrees of reality. To say that something is *real* is no more than a function of our language in saying that "There exists an x." Concerning a natural apple, we can say, "There exists an x such that x is an apple." Concerning the plastic apple, we can say, "There exists an x such that x is an apple and x is plastic." There is no need to appeal to degrees of *being, reality,* or *truth.* Questions about what is *real* boil down to questions about the way we use language.

Do you agree with Quine? Which philosopher makes better sense of your experience with a natural and an artificial object? Why?

COMPARE DOG BREEDS

Examine various breeds of dogs. If you are not a dog owner, go to a pet store or a public park where people walk their dogs. Notice how different one breed is from another. Some dogs, such as Great Danes, are extremely large; others, such as Chihuahuas, are very small. Some dogs have pointy ears; others have floppy ears. Some have long, extended, smooth snouts; others have short, wrinkled snouts. Big dogs tend to have a lower-pitched bark than small dogs. Cocker Spaniels are known as gentle dogs; Pit Bulls and German Shepherds are considered to be more aggressive.

Why are all these creatures that appear so different from one another labeled as "dogs"? It is quite a bit easier to think of mice as being members of the same species, since one mouse looks very similar to another mouse. The same can be said for chipmunks or rabbits. Human beings look alike; while a few people are dwarves or giants, they are the exception rather than the rule. Human faces, despite their differences, look about the same. But a bulldog's face does not look like a beagle's. So the question remains, why are all these animals that appear so differently from one another, *dogs?*"

Plato understood this problem. He believed that in the world of our senses we could not discover what a dog (or anything else) is in reality, because they vary too much from one another. We have to go beyond our senses and use reason. Through reason, we can understand the traits that are necessary for a dog to be a *dog*. For example, dogs are carnivorous mammals, they are pack animals, their genetic codes are similar enough for them to interbreed and so forth.

For Plato, however, using reason to discover the conditions essential for a dog to be a *dog* is not enough - what we are really attempting to discover is the *Form* of *Dogness*. The Form *Dogness* is not in space or time. It really exists in a separate world that transcends the world of our sense experience. It is unchanging and eternal. It is truly real, unlike the changing dogs that we experience in the world of our five senses. We can only know *Dogness* through reason, through a dialectical, question and answer method that brings us closer to discovering what is necessary for *Dogness*. For example, you might ask, *Is a particular color, such as brown, necessary for a dog to be a dog?* The proper reply is "no," since dogs, even those of the same breed, can have different colors. On the other hand, if you ask, *Is being carnivorous (being a meat-eater) necessary to be a dog*, the answer is "yes," since all breeds of dogs are meat-eaters. The more you know about what is essential to being a dog, the more you understand the Form *Dogness*.

Do you agree with Plato? Is the Form *Dogness* what is *really real?* What problems do you think he is trying to solve with his doctrine of the Forms? Is there some other way to solve these problems?

An alternative view is represented by Plato's student Aristotle. Aristotle believed in *forms* (with a small "f"), but he also believed that you cannot separate the form from the thing. So he thought the dogs you see and pet are *really real.* To determine what makes these creatures *dogs* as opposed to cats or mice, we use our sense experience and our power to understand what is universal to all dogs to separate the properties that are necessary to be a dog from those that are *accidental. Accidental* properties are properties such as hair color, size (although there will be a certain range of sizes - you do not find fifty foot long Dachshunds), and the pitch of a dog's bark. *Essential* properties are, for example, the particular genetic code of dogs as well as their being carnivorous mammals, and being (theoretically at least) able to breed with any other dog.

What do Plato and Aristotle have in common? How do they differ? Who do you believe has the best answer to the question, "What makes a dog a *dog?*"

PLAY WITH TIME

Read the following sentence:
The quick brown fox jumped over the lazy dog's back.
Before you read the sentence, the act of your reading it was in the future. While you were reading it, you were reading it in the present. Now that you have already read the sentence, the act of your reading it is now in the past.

Surely that is obvious. Don't we always divide our actions into those that have taken place in the past, those taking place now, and those that will take place in the future? What is so odd about that?

That was the first reaction of St. Augustine, Bishop of Hippo in North Africa, when he thought about time. Understanding time seems as easy as understanding the past, present and future of reading a sentence or of any other event. But when he tried to define time, Augustine found he was unable to do so. Try to define time yourself. Do you find the same difficulty?

Augustine eventually decided that time involved processes that occurred in the mind. This does not mean that time is unreal or an illusion. It does mean that time involves subjective mental processes. The past is something we remember. The present is what passes in our experience now. The future involves anticipation. According to Augustine's theory, when you read the italicized sentence above, you anticipated reading it - that was the future. You experienced reading it - that was the present. And now you remember reading it - that is the past. Do you agree with Augustine? Does his account make complete sense of the nature of time? Does it make sense of your experience of reading the italicized sentence?

The British philosopher John McTaggart (1866-1925) believed that time is unreal. He distinguished between what he labeled the *A series of time* and the *B series of time*. The *A series of time* is when we order events as past, present and future. The *B series of time* includes the notion that some events occur earlier or later than other events. However, it does not involve any language referring to *past*, *present* or *future*. McTaggart believes that to make sense of our concept of time, we must understand it in terms of the *A series*; that is, the concepts of *past*, *present* and *future* are

40

required in our understanding of time. Any event, such as your reading of the italicized sentence, must eventually be *past*, *present* and *future*. However, *past*, *present* and *future* do not refer to the same qualities. Thus, if an event is *past*, *present* and *future*, it has properties that contradict one another. Contradictions must be false. Therefore, time is unreal.

Do you agree with McTaggart? When you read the italicized sentence, was it essential that you would read it in the future, read it in the present and had read it in the past? If so, how can your reading the sentence be *past*, *present* and *future*? If you answer, "It can't be past, present and future at the same time," McTaggart would probably say that you are appealing to time, the very thing you are trying to explain. Do you agree?

EXAMINE A DEAD PLANT NEXT TO A LIVING ONE

What is life? What is the difference between a dead and living thing? Is it chemical? Does it involve a soul?

Go outside and pluck a plant, roots and all. Set it down for a day and then bring it outside to a living plant of the same kind. Are you able to tell what life is by doing that? Has the matter of the dead plant changed now that it is dead? Besides some withering, has the shape of the dead plant changed significantly? Is it chemical composition or shape that makes the difference between life and death?

Aristotle noted that if you place a freshly dead plant or animal beside a living one, it is not the material makeup of the dead thing that distinguishes it from a living thing. The freshly dead plant or animal has the same chemicals as a living plant or animal. Yes, the dead plant or animal no longer grows, and eventually it will decay, but Aristotle said that these were signs of something that has left the dead organism. What he believed has left a dead organism is the *soul*.

Today when we think of the word *soul* we think in terms of human beings, and in terms of some kind of nonmaterial part of us that interacts with the body. For Aristotle, the *soul* is the *form of the body*, and is the life-principle that organizes nonliving matter into a living being. It is the wholeness that is more than the sum of the parts of a living thing. Aristotle believed that not only humans have souls but also nonhuman animals and even plants. Humans only have a *rational soul* that is responsible for their ability to reason as well as their abilities to sense, feel emotions, be nourished and grow. Animals have a *sensitive soul* that gives the animal the power of sensation, emotions and self-movement as well as the powers of nutrition and growth. Plants have a *nutritive* or *vegetative soul* that gives the plant the power of nutrition and growth.

When the matter of a body becomes damaged severely enough, the soul, the life force and organizing principle, cannot remain in the body, and the soul separates from the body. For Aristotle, when plant and animal souls separate, not only does this eventually lead to the corruption of the body, but the soul is corrupted as well. It is hard to say what Aristotle believes about human souls after death, but it is nearly certain that he did not believe in an individual separated human soul retaining its

42

individual identity after death.

Does Aristotle's view make sense to you? Is what makes the living plant you saw alive its *soul*? When the plant you plucked died, was this due to its soul separating from the plant and corrupting?

Charles Darwin (1809-1882), the British naturalist most famous for the development of the theory of evolution by natural selection, disagrees with Aristotle. Unlike Aristotle, Darwin was a *reductionist*; that is, he believed that life could be reduced to the interactions of the chemical elements within the organism and ultimately be reduced to the laws of physics. There is no room, Darwin believed, for any kind of *soul, form of the body*, or *life force*.

Do you believe Darwin is right? Is life an advanced group of chemical reactions and nothing more? Do you agree with this view given your experiment with the living and dead plant?

Start a Domino Chain

Have you wondered whether the next time you drop a ball, gravity will cause it to fall to the earth? Most people take a regular order of cause and effect for granted. They assume that if they put salt on food, the salt will not suddenly change into a deadly poison and cause their death. They assume if they hit a cue ball with a cue stick the blow will cause the ball to roll.

Line up a group of dominos. They should be near enough to one another so that if you tip one domino the others will fall as well. Now tip the first domino and watch the others fall. Does it seem that one domino hitting the next one causes it to fall, and the process of cause and effect continues until all the dominos fall? Do you believe there is a *necessary* relationship between cause and effect? That is, when one domino hits another domino, is it necessary that it affect the other domino's motion?

The Scottish philosopher David Hume believed that there is no necessary connection between cause and effect. He was an empiricist; that is, he believed any knowledge we have of the world has to come from sense experience. He claimed that cause and effect involves three components. First, the objects involved must be near each other in space and time. Hume called this *contiguity in space and time*. He takes this belief from the classical, Newtonian physics of his day. Was that true in your domino experiment? Did the dominos have to be near one other in space and time?

Second, we experience a *constant conjunction* of cause and effect. Both in our past memories of causes and effects and when we are actually looking at a cause and effect relationship, we see that the same cause always produces the same or similar effect. Repeat your domino experiment several times. Does one domino still tip over other dominos?

However, Hume did not believe that there is a *necessary connection* between cause and effect. Reason fails to inform us about any such connection, and to have *sense experience* of *necessary connection*, we would have to know the future. Can you know the future by experience? Is it possible for you to see the dominos falling in future experiments? Or is your *sense experience* only of the past (via memory) and the present (via direct sensation)? If so, how can you know in the future that tipping the first domino will always and necessarily cause the next domino to fall? Hume says you cannot know this. Is he right?

Alfred North Whitehead, a British philosopher who moved to the United States and taught at Harvard University, disagreed with Hume. He believed that we actually perceive a connection between cause and effect, something he called *causal efficacy*. This is a kind of perception that does not occur through our five senses. It is similar to the perception we have of the internal processes of our own bodies. We sense that our bodies are alive and functioning even if we are not aware of such functioning via the five senses. In a similar way, we sense a regular connection between cause and effect even if that perception is not via the five senses. Is that true? Did you somehow sense that the first domino was actually causing the next domino to fall? Is Whitehead's position a good reply to Hume?

WRITE A LETTER TO SANTA CLAUS

Did you ever write letters to Santa Claus as a child? Did you really believe that Santa lived at the North Pole with Mrs. Claus and the elves and rode a Sleigh on Christmas Eve led by eight reindeer (and maybe a ninth, Rudolph)? How did it feel when you discovered that Santa Claus does not actually exist?

For a moment, pretend you never heard the news that there is no Santa. Write a letter to Santa Claus. As you did as a child, ask him for whatever you want for Christmas.

How did you feel writing such a letter? Did you feel silly or childish, or did part of you wonder if Santa Claus really exists somewhere? Could there be some universe in which Santa lives at the North Pole and gives presents to all the good girls and boys on Christmas Eve?

David Lewis (1941-2001), who was Professor of Philosophy at Princeton University, wrote extensively about possible worlds. We live in the actual world. Since it is actual, it is obviously possible as well. But there might be another world that differs either slightly or a great deal from this one. For example, one possible world is one in which George H. W. Bush defeated Bill Clinton and served a second term. That world is not the actual world, but since there is no logical contradiction in supposing that Mr. Bush defeated Mr. Clinton, it is a possible world.

Another possible world is one in which Santa Claus exists. There does not seem to be a logical contradiction in the notion of Santa Claus or in the existence of elves and flying reindeer if the physical laws of that world are different than this one. That world is not our actual world - but could it really exist in some other universe?

Lewis believed that possible worlds are just as real as the actual world. The word *modal* refers to possibility and necessity, so Lewis' view is called *modal realism*. He believes that the only thing that makes the *actual world* actual is the fact that we are the ones living in it (the technical way of putting it is to say that "actual world" is an *indexical* term). There are an infinite number of real possible worlds, all separated from one another in space and time. We can know something about them by combining categories from the actual world. For example, there are reindeer (caribou) in the actual world. There are also creatures that fly (birds, bats).

Combine "reindeer" and "flying," and you get "flying reindeer." Play around with other categories in the actual world until you can come up with "elves" and "Santa Claus."

It would follow that there really is a world in which George H. W. Bush defeated Bill Clinton, and there really is a world in which Santa Claus exists and children write letters to a real person. Do you agree with Lewis? Perhaps there is a world in which someone identical or almost identical to you is writing a letter to Santa Claus - and in that world a real Santa will read the letter!

Alvin Plantinga (1932-), who teaches philosophy at the University of Notre Dame, does not agree that possible worlds really exist. He prefers the word *state of affairs* to the word *world*. Plantinga believes that the difference between a possible world and the actual world is that in the actual world the states of affairs that make it up *obtain*, that is, statements about them are true. Thus, it is true to say "Bill Clinton won the U.S. presidential election in 1992." It is also true to say "There is no Santa Claus." However, there are other states of affairs that, while not impossible, are false and *do not obtain*. For example, it is false to say that "George H. W. Bush won the 1992 U.S. presidential election." It is false to say that "Santa Claus really exists."

Do you agree with Plantinga? Would it make a difference in your attitude toward writing your letter to Santa Claus if Plantinga were wrong and Lewis were right?

PULL OUT ONE HAIR

How much would have to change about you to make you a different individual? How much would your personality, values or appearance have to change? Pull one hair from your head, or if that is too uncomfortable, cut one hair with scissors. Now suppose you had not pulled or cut that hair. Would you have been a different individual?

Gottfried Leibniz, the great German philosopher who discovered the calculus about the same time as Sir Isaac Newton in England, believed you would have been a different individual entirely if you had not pulled or cut the hair. Leibniz believed that everything about your appearance, your personality, every event in your life, is necessary. The only reason you do not see that these things are necessary is because your knowledge is limited, but God has a perfect understanding of you in His mind. Thus, if you pulled or cut a hair for this exercise, this is necessarily a part of what makes you *you*. The notion that literally everything has to be the same for something to be itself is called the *indiscernibility of identicals*.

It follows that if you had been born one microsecond later or earlier than you were, you would be a completely different person. If your heart had beat 70 times the previous minute instead of 69, then you would have been a completely different person. If you had pulled a different hair than the one you pulled, you would have been a completely different person. Is Leibniz right? Was it a necessary part of who you are that you followed this exercise and removed one hair from your head? Do you think this matters for your identity, or do you believe it to be trivial? Why?

Saul Kripke (1940-) taught philosophy at Princeton University and is now Distinguished Professor of Philosophy at the Graduate School of the City University of New York. He is discussing reference rather than identity, but we shall see that his position has implications for identity. What does it mean to refer to someone or something? For example, people once believed that George Washington chopped down a cherry tree. It turns out that event almost certainly did not take place. Yet we still call the first president of the United States *George Washington*. Why should we do this?

Kripke believes that once a community gives a name to a person, animal or object, that individual has received something like *an initial baptism*. Once a name is given, the name becomes what Kripke calls *a rigid designator*. That is, once the baby *George Washington* is named, we can refer to that individual as *George Washington in all possible worlds*. So if George Washington had not served in the French and Indian War, he still would be George Washington. And it certainly wouldn't matter whether he'd pulled one hair off his head on January 29, 1798, at 6:11 p.m.

If Kripke is right, it does not matter for who you are whether you removed or did not remove one hair from your head at a certain time. It does not even matter if you chose a different college or grew up in a different location. It is the *initial baptism* of your being given a name that makes it possible for people to refer to you as the same individual despite different possible histories.

Is Kripke right? Is it possible that he downplays events in your life as important for making you the person you are? Or is he correct that such events do not matter for the individual called *Your Name*. Do you believe that both Leibniz and Kripke are wrong and that some other account must be given of your identity through time? If so, what account would you give?

Shut the Door to Your Room
When You are not Inside It

Does the world exist outside your own mind? The answer may seem obvious to you, but it was not so obvious to some of the most significant philosophers in history. When you are alone in your room, walk outside your room and shut the door. Do you believe that the things you saw in your room earlier continue to exist when you are not observing them? If so, on what basis do you believe this?

Now open the door and look inside. Do things seem to be the same as before? Walk around and check where items are. Has any object disappeared or has any object moved? What do you think the results of your experiment prove?

John Stuart Mill (1806-1873), known primarily for his work on ethics, also did work in epistemology. He argued that you cannot know that the objects in your room remain there as actual objects when you (or someone else) is not observing them. He believed that when you are not observing an object, it continues to exist as *a permanent possibility of sensation*. For example, suppose one of the objects you observed before you closed the door to your room was your desk. Mill believes that when you leave the room, the desk continues to exist as a *permanent possibility of various sensations*. *If* you were standing six feet from the desk at a certain angle, you *would* see a certain rectangular shape. If you were at a different angle, the shape would be different. *If* you tapped the desk with your fingers, you *would* hear a particular sound. The actual desk does not exist outside your perception except as these kinds of possibilities.

Is Mill correct? Do your desk and the other objects in your room lose their full actuality and turn into possibilities when you are not observing them? Why or why not?

John Locke believes that everything in your room continues to exist when you are not observing it. Unlike Mill, he accepts the doctrine of material substance. *Substance*, to Locke, is what underlies qualities such as mass and shape. We are unable to perceive the substance itself; it is a "something, I know not what." Substance is what upholds the qualities that are literally in the object, the primary qualities, such as extension and mass. When you closed the door to your room, the objects in the room remained as extended material substances with a particular mass. Do you agree with Locke? Does it make sense to think that substance is a "something, I know not what?" If Locke's view is incorrect, must Mill's position be the only other option?

THROW A BALL AND WATCH IT FLY THROUGH THE AIR

The notion that objects stay the same is something we take for granted. But should we take this for granted? After all, the world is changing constantly, even when we are not aware of it. Atoms and molecules move on my desk and on yours as well. You accidentally scratch your desk and the scratch is an attribute it did not have before. You make a paper airplane and it changes because it is moving.

Take a ball and throw it into the air. It can be any kind of ball that's safe to throw, such as a football or soccer ball, or a smaller ball. Watch it as it flies along its path and falls to the ground. Is it the same ball throughout the flight?

Gottfried Wilhelm Leibniz did not believe that an object in flight is the same object throughout. In his view, the ball in flight is really a series of balls, each one created anew by God at each instant while the ball is in the air. Since this creation of new balls is continuous, it appears to you that one and the same ball had a smooth path in flight. But this is illusory.

Do you agree with Leibniz? Could any evidence from your senses serve to disprove Leibniz? Does it matter if such evidence is lacking?

The German philosopher Immanuel Kant believed that the notion of a continuing substance is a structure in our minds - but a necessary structure. If we did not experience the world as a succession of stable substances moving through time, the world would be chaotic, and meaningful experience would be impossible. In the case of the ball's flight, in order to make sense of that experience, we must already have, as part of our *mental equipment*, a notion that the ball is the same ball throughout its flight. This does not mean, Kant believes, that we know that the ball really is the same ball throughout its flight. That would mean knowing what the ball is in itself apart from our experience, and such knowledge of what Kant labels the *noumenal world* is impossible. The ball may be the same substance *really*, or it may not be. What is important is that we have to experience it as the same substance to experience its flight.

Given your experience of watching the ball in flight, between the two philosophers, do you agree more with Leibniz or with Kant? Is there a position other than those two you would like to defend? If so, which one and how would you defend it?

IMAGINE THAT WHAT IS HAPPENING TO YOU NOW HAPPENED BEFORE

Have you ever had a sense that what you are doing right now happened before? Try to create that experience now. Try convincing yourself that what you are doing now has happened before in exactly the same way. Then expand that vision. Pretend every event in your life has occurred before. This should not involve reincarnation, the belief that your soul will be reincarnated in a different body after you die. You should pretend an *identical you* experienced exactly the same events in life as you have experienced, are experiencing and will experience in the future. Now assume that the same thing is true of your friends. Expand that to the other people in the world, to the animals and plants, then to the universe itself. Pretend everything that has happened, is happening and will happen in this universe, has happened before.

Friedrich Nietzsche, a German philosopher, accepted the notion of an *eternal return*. That is, everything that has happened repeats itself over and over in an endless cycle. Although it is uncertain how literally Nietzsche took the *eternal return*, let us take it as a serious theory of what reality is really like. Does it make sense to you? Can you imagine a world in which everything that happens has happened before? Even if you can imagine such a world, does that mean that an *eternal return* is plausible? Why or why not?

Eudemos of Rhodes (c. 350-c. 490 B.C.), a student of Aristotle, was responding to an earlier doctrine of *eternal return* he believed the Pythagoreans taught. In his response, Eudemos suggested that an *eternal return* is impossible. Literally the same events cannot repeat themselves, since they would no longer be the *same* events. Occurring at a specific time is as much a part of an event as what happens at that time. If I blow my nose today and do the same thing twenty billion years from now, the second act must be a different one from the first since they occur at different times and cannot be numerically identical. Thus, a literal repetition of the exact same event involves a contradiction.

Is Eudemos correct that an *eternal return*, or even a literal repetition of one event, is impossible? Or is Nietzsche correct that it is possible. Does the exercise of imagining that what has happened to you happened before affect your answer?

PLACE THREE APPLES SIDE BY SIDE

We human beings classify things quite a bit, don't we? We see several trees that produce acorns and classify them as *oaks*. We look at a German Shepherd and a Pomeranian and call them both *dogs*. But to what are we referring when we label a set of trees *oaks*, or several dogs of different types as *dogs*? Is there a basis in reality for how we use those words, or is it just a matter of convention or habit?

Place three apples (or oranges or tomatoes, as long as the three objects are of the same kind) side by side. Preferably the apples will be of different colors, like Granny Smith and Red Delicious. Compare them. What do they have in common? How are they different? Why do you call each of the objects by one name - if you have three apples side by side, why do you call them apples?

Nelson Goodman (1906-1998), an American philosopher who taught for many years at Harvard University, did not believe that words such as *apple* or *orange* referred to real similarities between apples and oranges - they are convenient labels we use in language to identify objects we take to be similar. His position is an extreme form of *nominalism*, the theory that universal words such as *apple* and *oak* only refer to individual things. Universal classes, such as *apple* and *oak* only have reality in our language. They do not refer to anything real outside our use of words.

Is Goodman correct? Are there any similarities between apples themselves that make them *apples*, even apart from our words?

Aristotle held a different position. He believed that objects we call apples have the nature of *appleness*. Rather than *appleness* existing in a separate world of its own, as Aristotle's teacher Plato believed, Aristotle thought that *appleness* exists in each individual apple. Apples are really alike. They would be alike even if there were no humans to use language to label them as *apples*. Aristotle's position is known as *moderate realism*. It is *realism* because he believes in real natures such as *appleness* or *oakness*. But, unlike Plato's extreme realism, Aristotle is *moderate* because he believes that natures exist in individual things.

Given the results of your experiment, do you agree more with Aristotle or with Goodman?

EXAMINE A PIECE OF GRANITE

Is a piece of granite, or any other rock, lifeless? That is something we take for granted. However, not every philosopher agrees with that view. Pick up a piece of granite. If you are unable to find granite, pick up another kind of rock. Examine the rock closely. If you are examining granite and have something that can chip off the individual minerals - quartz, feldspar, mica - use it and examine the pieces. Does the granite seem alive? Or is it a mere inert object without life and mind?

Gottfried Leibniz did not believe matter, including rocks such as granite, was lifeless, even though they may appear so to us. He believed that every *material* object is built out of *monads*. These are *bits of mind* that *perceive* the world (this does not imply that all monads have *conscious* perception, what he labels *apperception*) from their own unique perspective. Each monad is *windowless*; that is, no monad is externally related to another monad. They *work together* in the sense that God pre-programs them so that they harmonize and produce the world of our experience, including granite, trees and human beings. Even a rock is ultimately made of *mind-stuff* - the theory that everything in the universe is made of mind is called *panpsychism - pan* for "all" and *psychism* for "mind." Each piece of quartz, mica and feldspar is made of monads, and so is the piece of granite as a whole. You are made of monads as well; your soul or mind, which does consciously perceive, is your most important monad.

Is Leibniz correct that even a piece of rock such as granite is made of mind? Why or why not?

Leibniz was reacting against the view of René Descartes. Descartes believed that matter was passive, inert and lifeless. A rock such as granite is completely mindless. Matter is defined in terms of extension in space. Only God and human souls (and perhaps angels) are minds. The rest of the universe is *dead*. Although his view seems to make sense, Leibniz thought it made too sharp a distinction between mind and matter, and he also wondered how passive, dead matter could do anything at all. Which view makes more sense to you regarding the piece of granite: Leibniz's or Descartes'? Why?

WRITE DOWN YOUR EARLIEST MEMORIES

Could you imagine yourself as the same person now as ten years ago if you had no memories? Do you believe that you are the same person over time? If so, are memories part of what you believe makes you the same person as you were in the past?

Write down your earliest memories. How old were you? What happened? How many gaps are there between your earliest memories and the next things you remember? Do you think it is possible that five years ago you may have remembered things that happened in the past that you have now forgotten?

John Locke was an English philosopher who was the first of the *British Empiricists*. He believed that we gain knowledge of the world by means of our five senses. We record past experiences of what we sense through our memories. A stream of memories also points to something Locke believed is even more important: a continuous stream of consciousness going back through time. Consciousness is what makes human beings persons, Locke thought, rather than mere animals. You are the same person now as you were five or ten years ago because your consciousness goes back that far. But the only way you can know that your consciousness goes back that far is through your memories of the past. Personal identity through time, then, arises from a stream of memories through time.

Do you agree with Locke that your memories are what make you the same person in the past as you are now? What if there are gaps in your memory? Does that make a difference? Do gaps in your memory mean that you are never the same person through time? What if at age five you remembered something you did when you were three that you have forgotten now? Would that change your past identity?

Another English philosopher, who also served as Anglican Bishop of Durham, Joseph Butler (1692-1752), disagreed with Locke's memory criterion for personal identity. He argued that memory presupposes that a person already exists, rather than being the basis of personal identity. Locke, therefore, *puts the cart before the horse*. You already have to exist as a person to have even your first memory, so memory cannot be what makes you a person. Is Butler correct? If so, and memory is not what gives you personal identity, what does? If you cannot find an alternative theory of personal identity, does this imply that there is no such thing as being the same person over time? Why or why not?

DO NOTHING FOR FIFTEEN MINUTES
THEN DO SOMETHING YOU ENJOY FOR FIFTEEN MINUTES

Have you ever been bored? Did time seem to pass slowly then? When you do something you enjoy, does time seem to speed up? Get a stopwatch or mark the time on your own watch. Do absolutely nothing for fifteen minutes. How slowly did time seem to pass? Now do something you enjoy for fifteen minutes. Did time still pass slowly or did it seem to pass more quickly? What does your experience mean for the nature of time?

Augustine believed that our experience of the passage of time depends on our subjective experience. Time may seem at some points to pass slowly and at other points to pass quickly. This does not mean that time is unreal; it only implies that the passage of time is dependent on our conscious experience, and that depends on a number of factors. Our sense of time may be influenced by pain (time may seem to pass more slowly when you're hurting) or pleasure (in intense pleasure, such as deep enjoyment of a piece of music or sexual climax, the sense of time passing may disappear). How could you apply Augustine's view of time to your own experiment? Does it fit what happened to you? Does this mean Augustine is right about the nature of time?

Parmenides (fl. 5th century B.C.) was an ancient Greek philosopher who worked on the Island of Elea. He did not accept the reality of time; the universe, he believed, is an *undifferentiated unity* - that is, it has no parts. Since time implies division - one time passes by to be replaced by another and so forth - time is unreal. If the results of your experiment were that time flows at different speeds depending on what you are doing, Parmenides would most likely interpret those results as implying that time is an illusion. After all, if time is real, shouldn't it be something that flows at the same rate? Does Parmenides make sense of your experience? Does using the watch to time yourself make any difference? Could there be an alternative way to explain time other than those of Augustine and Parmenides? If so, what?

THINK ABOUT REDNESS

I s it possible to have a general idea, such as an idea of *dogness* or *square-shaped*? What about a color? For a few moments, think about *redness*. What do you experience? Do you have a sense that the concept *red* was in your mind? Do you see a vast red expanse? Or do you imagine a particular red object? Do you have an image in your mind at all?

John Locke, the first member of a group of philosophers called *the British Empiricists*, believed that it is possible to have general ideas. We form general ideas by a method Locke called *abstraction*. Here is how it works. To come up with a general idea of *dog*, remove all characteristics that belong to a particular dog. All that remains are characteristics that belong to all dogs. The same method can be applied to the color red. To come up with a general idea of *redness*, think of redness in general, not a particular red object. Remove all other characteristics other than the color red, and you will be left with a general idea of *redness*.

Does Locke's theory match your experience of *redness*? Were you able to remove all particular red things from your mind? When you thought about *redness*, did you think about it without an image of *red* in your mind? Is your answer significant in your evaluation of Locke's theory?

The second of the British Empiricists, the Irish philosopher George Berkeley, did not believe it is possible for us to formulate general ideas. Instead, he believed that all ideas in the mind are of particular things. If you try to form a general idea of *dogness*, what you will think about is an individual dog of a particular shape, size and breed (even if it is a mutt). If you try to formulate a general idea of *redness*, you will think about a particular shade of red rather than *redness* in general. It is important that Berkeley thought Locke believed all ideas are images in the mind.

Does Berkeley's theory fit your experience better than Locke's? If Locke believed all ideas are images, does this pose a problem for his theory? If he did not believe that, do Berkeley's criticisms work? How does your own experience in thinking about *redness* make a difference in your answer?

VISIT AN UNFAMILIAR TOWN

Have you ever felt out of place in the world? Maybe home does not seem like home and you feel as if you are a stranger in the world. If you have never felt this way, have you ever felt out of place in an unfamiliar setting? Try to remember your first trip to town as a child or your first visit to a new friend's house. There may have been times in your life in which you found yourself in a place you did not ask to be. For example, your parents may have taken you to the store to buy shoes when you had planned to play baseball with your friends. Did you feel trapped in the store, caught there with no way out?

Visit an unfamiliar town. It does not have to be far from your home, only a place you have never seen before, not even in photos. When you drive across the town limits, do you feel disoriented or strange that you are in a new place? Now give a friend a list of nearby towns you have never visited. Have your friend choose one of those towns and take you there. Did you feel lost or disoriented then? If so, were you more disoriented than when you visited a town by your own choice?

Martin Heidegger was a German philosopher and one of the most important philosophers of the twentieth century. He believed that we do not feel at home in the world. We did not ask to be born, we did not ask to be placed on this earth; it is as if we have been *thrown* into the world. This sense of *throwness* (*Geworfenheit*) causes us to feel anxious, especially since our ultimate fate in an unfamiliar world is death. Even though we can find some sense of identity by choosing to live authentically, rather than by following the crowd, we are never really at home in the world. Jim Morrison (1943-1971), lead singer of the rock group *The Doors*, sang out the words of "Riders on the Storm"

Riders on the storm
Riders on the storm
Into this house we're born
Into this world we're thrown
Like a dog without a bone
An actor out of role
Riders on the storm

Those words express Heidegger's thoughts exactly - instead of feeling at home in the world, our visit here is very much like a visit to an unfamiliar town. Is that how you feel about your life in the world? Are Heidegger and Morrison correct? Why or why not?

Stuart Kauffman (1939-), who was a professor at the University of Calgary and now is at the University of Vermont, believes that the universe is a fitting home for human beings. He believes that the universe is a self-organizing system that naturally brought forth complex organisms such as ourselves. The self-organization was not a conscious process, and there is no creator God involved. But we are not out of place in this world; we developed as part of the world, and we are made to live in this world. Rather than being *thrown* into an alien land, we belong here.

Do you agree with Kauffman's position that we developed as part of this world and that this world is therefore our home? Do you think science can solve the problem of whether the world is our home? Does the world seem more like a strange town or do you believe you fit into the world like a hand in a glove?

WATCH A DOG FOLLOW A SCENT

How smart are animals? Do they run on pure instinct or are they capable of reasoning? Or are humans the only animals with the capacity for reason?

If you own a dog or know someone who owns one, watch the dog when it follows a scent. Hunting dogs are especially good at this. If you do not have access to a dog, rent a documentary about dog behavior and observe the dog as it hunts its prey. How does the dog behave? Does it check out alternative paths? Does it choose the correct path by reasoning of some kind or does it follow a scent blindly by instinct? What is it about the dog's behavior that supports your conclusion?

The ancient Stoic philosopher Chrysippus (280-206 B.C.) argued that animals can reason. He used the following example. A dog is trying to cross a road to follow the scent of prey. But the road has three exits. Suppose the dog checks exit A, then exit B but finally follows exit C. Chrysippus claims that the dog is using reason to reach a conclusion in this way: The correct path is either through exit A or B or C. It is not through exits A or B; therefore, it must be via exit C. This involves a classic rule of logic known as *disjunctive syllogism*, which in its simplest form goes *A or B; not A; therefore B*. You can see that the above example is just a more complicated use of the rule.

Does the dog finding the correct exit really use a standard rule of logic in doing so? Is the dog using reason? From your observations of a dog tracking a scent, what do you think?

Philo (20 B.C.-50 A.D.) was a Jewish philosopher who lived in Alexandria, Egypt. He believed that Chrysippus' argument does not prove that the dog is using reason to find the correct exit. Rather, the dog is using the sense of smell to follow a scent, and there is no need to claim that it is reasoning. It is simply following its sense of smell.

From your observation of the dog tracking a scent, who is closer to the truth about animal reasoning: Chrysippus or Philo? Could there be a third position between the two philosophers about the role of sensation and reason in the dog's behavior?

FIND SOME RANDOM ROCKS

Does everything have a reason? Some people believe that there is a reason for their lives. Is there a reason, however, for everything else being the way it is? Is anything truly random in the universe?

Find a place where there are some small rocks and focus on a few of them at random. Do not pick them up. Is there a reason that they must be in the place they are? Or did they find their way to that place randomly?

Gottfried Leibniz did not believe in randomness in the universe. Instead, he believed that every object and every event has a sufficient reason for being the way it is. There are no attributes of an object that are not necessary to it. Size, shape, color, location in space - all those properties are just as necessary for an object's identity as its chemical formula. The object itself and all its properties must have sufficient reasons for their existence.

Take the rocks, for instance. Leibniz believed there must be a sufficient reason for their existence and a sufficient reason for all their properties, including the place they are located. Everything happens by necessity. As humans, we are not able to see this necessity in most cases because the world is so complex. But God knows the sufficient reason for everything, including the reason for everything about the rocks.

Do you agree with Leibniz that there is nothing random about the rocks you observed? Do you agree that there must be a sufficient reason for every property of the rocks, including where they are, every chip on them, their size, etc.? Or is there some randomness about them? If so, what?

Democritus (460-370 B.C.) was an ancient Greek philosopher who, with Leucippus (fl. 5th century B.C.) developed a doctrine called *atomism*. He believed that everything in the world is made of indivisible atoms. Atoms run into each other by chance and make up everything in the world. There is no sufficient reason for things being the way they are; where an atom or group of atoms ends up is a matter of where they happen to fall and to which atoms they stick. In the case of the rocks, groups of atoms happened to stick together to form them. Some atoms have sloughed off due to erosion. Random motion of water and earth led to the rocks being where they are.

Do you agree with Democritus that the rocks just happen to be the way they are and where they are due to random collisions of atoms? Does his view make more sense than the view that everything about them has a sufficient reason? Why or why not?

STEP TWO TIMES INTO FLOWING WATER

There is an old saying that states, "The only constant in life is change." Has that been true of your life? Is there anything you notice strange about the old saying? What about the two words *change* and *constant* being together in the same sentence? Does this cause a problem?

Put one foot into a body of moving water, such as a creek, branch or river. (Be sure it is in a shallow place for your own safety). Now put the other foot into the water. Step back onto the shore and repeat. Is the body of water you stepped in with one foot the same body of water that flowed past your other? When you stepped back into the body of water, is it the same body of water you stepped in the first time?

The ancient Greek philosopher Heraclitus (535-475 B.C.) is one of the *Presocratic Philosophers* because he wrote his work before the great Greek philosopher Socrates. Heraclitus' most famous statement is "You cannot step into the same river twice." Why does he say this? Because *different waters flow* in the river. By the time you step into the river the second time, the water that washed your feet has already passed, and you are feeling *new* water. The river is not the same river from moment to moment. Thus, change is constant in nature (although Heraclitus also believes that Logos, what we would call today *natural law*, keeps change orderly).

Is Heraclitus correct? Can you step into the same body of water twice? Is the body of water you stepped into the same body of water over time?

The famous student of Socrates, Plato, was disturbed by Heraclitus' claim, and more disturbed by the claim of Heraclitus' follower Cratylus (late 5th century B.C.), who said you can't even step into the same river *once*. Yet if that is true, how can we know anything at all about rivers or other things in the world? If all is change with no stability, then we could not even name things.

Plato solved the problem with his doctrine of the Forms. Although our five senses reveal a world of constant change, our intellect can penetrate into the *essence* of things. The *essence* is what makes a thing what it is. By understanding the *essence*, our minds understand something about the Form. The Form, *Riverness*, does not exist on the earth; it exists in a transcendent realm, in another world, and is unchanging and eternal. Because it is unchanging, we can understand what a river is. And a river or other body of water on earth maintains some level of stability because it *participates* in the Form of Riverness. In a sense, then, you *can* step into the same river twice.

Is Plato correct in believing that the doctrine of the Forms can deal with Heraclitus' and Cratylus' problems? Could there be another way to support the idea that the river is the same river over time?

LISTEN TO A PIECE OF MUSIC, THEN LOOK AT MUSICAL NOTES IN A SONGBOOK

D o you like music? Most of us do, although we may not like the same kinds of music. When you listen to music, can you distinguish individual notes? If you do not know how to read music, that might be difficult, but is it easier if you do? Now look at the musical notes in a songbook. They represent individual units of sound. Is experiencing the individual sounds the experience you have when you listen to music?

David Hume believed that anything occurring in time, such as music, is divided into discrete, indivisible units, something like atoms. Is his view adequate to your experience of listening to music? Does music *sound* like a group of individual, indivisible *atoms of sound*, each one passing the other? When you heard music, did *atoms* of music pass into the past? Did new *atoms* of music replace them in the present? Did you expect more *atoms* of music as the song or piece of music continued? Is music that *choppy*, or do you experience it as a flow without discrete units, more like the flow of water in a river?

One of the greatest American philosophers, who also contributed to psychology, was William James (1842-1910). James believed that events in time flow rather than pass by in atomic units. We experience the world in terms of a *specious present*, in which the past passes smoothly into the present and the present passes smoothly into the future, like the flow of a river. Is this how you experienced listening to a piece of music? Did it flow smoothly in the present to the point that you were not aware of notes being in the past or future, but of the musical piece as a developing whole? Or was music more like billiard balls hitting other billiard balls (Hume)?

OBSERVE A DESK

Do you take it for granted that the world of your sense experience is the real world? When you observe an object, do you assume that it exists exactly the way you see it, or at least close?

Observe a desk. Do not just look at it, but feel its texture, listen to the sounds it makes when you tap it. Is it really solid? Does it really have the texture you feel when you sweep its surface with your hand?

Bertrand Russell, a British philosopher primarily known for his work in the philosophy of mathematics and in the philosophy of language, questioned whether the desk we observe is the real desk. Science tells us, Russell says, that the desk is primarily empty space. It is made of atoms and molecules, but the vast majority of the desk is not *solid*. The color of the desk is due to the wavelength of light not absorbed by the desk. It is not actually part of the desk. The texture is due to the way our nervous system reacts to the molecular structure of the desk. Even though the desk looks the same over time, it is really constantly changing. Someone scratches the desk, modifying the shape. Someone cuts graffiti into it, cutting away some of the wood. Plus, natural processes may erode the desk too. So what seems like a stable, solid object really is not. The world of science shows us that we cannot trust our senses to tell us the real nature of the desk.

Do you agree with Russell? Does science keep us from knowing the real nature of things with our unaided senses?

Aristotle was a *direct realist*. That is, he believed that we know things in nature as they are in reality in a direct way through our senses. For Aristotle, the desk is real - it has a certain form and purpose. Even though the form and function are made by humans, the desk still has a form, albeit an artificial one. Of course we can talk about the form of the wood and the varnish that help make up the desk. However, the issue is the nature of the desk and whether we can know it really is a desk and its properties - and we can. As far as the wood is concerned, it is solid, whether it is, from a scientific point of view, made of empty space or not. Things have a wholeness that is more than the sum of their parts.

Is Aristotle correct? From your experience of observing the desk, which philosopher makes the most sense to you?

Philosophy of Mind

IMAGINE YOURSELF AS A DISEMBODIED SOUL

Have you ever wondered what it would be like to live without a body? Now is your chance to imagine what that experience would be. Sit in a dark room. Relax as much as possible and clear your mind of distractions. Imagine you have no eyes, no ears, no nose, no sense of touch, no sense organs or nervous system. You do not have a body at all. Are you still able to see? Can you hear? Can you reach out and touch something or someone? Can you smell any odors? Are you able to travel through space? Do you feel yourself floating? If so, *what* is floating? Can you float through three-dimensional space without a body?

René Descartes believed that a disembodied soul could have experiences, feelings, thoughts and even perceptions. He was a dualist who believed that in this life human beings are composed of two different substances: *body*, which is extended in space and can be measured, and *soul*, which is not in space and cannot be measured. The body cannot think, feel or perceive without a soul; all of what makes you who you truly are is found in the soul. Since the soul is not a material object, it cannot break down into parts and thus cannot die or decay. It is not handicapped when it exists without a body; it can perform all its activities just as well as before.

Is Descartes correct in his belief that a disembodied soul has similar ways of thinking, feeling and experiencing as an embodied soul? Does the thought experiment change your position? If some of your friends try the experiment, how does their experience compare to yours? Do they agree or disagree with Descartes? Talk with your friends, and together try to discover any flaws in the arguments all of you present.

Epicurus was the founder of the Epicurean school of philosophy. The Epicureans followed the work of an earlier philosopher, Democritus, and believed that the soul fills the entire body, and like the body, it is made of tiny material particles called *atoms*. Although the soul's atoms are finer than the other atoms in the body, they are still material objects, and the soul, therefore, is not fundamentally different than the body. However, the soul cannot exist without the full body being present, and when a human body dies, the atoms making up the soul are dispersed into the air. A disembodied soul could have no experiences; what existence it could have would be fleeting as it flies apart after an individual's death.

Do you agree with Epicurus? Is there some other position other than Descartes' or Epicurus' that makes better sense of a disembodied soul? Did your thought experiment change your views from what they were previously?

DESCRIBE YOURSELF IN MEDICAL TERMS

When you think of who you really are, where does your body fit in? If you have a copy of your medical records, read your physician's narrative from your last examination. If not, do some research and then write down how a doctor might describe you using only medical terminology.

Does the physician's description match how you would describe your body? Is there anything important about your body that is missing from that description? Is biology the only correct way to describe your body? Is a medical, *scientific* description of your body better than other ways of describing it?

Now write a description, using ordinary language, about your visiting a grocery store. Describe what you do when you visit the store, from examining items and taking items off the shelf to paying the cashier. Then examine how you describe the activity of your body while you shopped. Are there differences between the language you use to describe your grocery store trip and the language the doctor used to describe you? If so, what are those differences?

René Descartes accepted *dualism*, the view that the human person is composed of two separate substances, a soul and a body. The soul is a thinking thing unextended in space, and the body is an unthinking thing extended in space. Although the soul and body interact in this life, the body is really nothing more than a machine.

For Descartes, the most accurate way of describing your body is by using scientific language. Such *clinical, objective*, language is more accurate than language about *how you feel*, since language about feelings is subjective and limited to the realm of the soul.

Do you agree with Descartes? Is clinical language, the language of test results, the best way to describe your body? Even apart from the issue of whether the doctor should pay attention to your feelings, is there something important about your body that Descartes misses? How much does your paragraph about a grocery trip square with Descartes' position?

Maurice Merleau-Ponty (1908-1961), who was, like Descartes, a French philosopher, disagreed with Descartes' clinical view of the human body. He focused on the *lived body* of our everyday experience. When you walk, for instance, you normally would not say, "My body is walking," or "My feet and legs are walking." Rather, you say, "I am walking." If you speak, you normally would not say, "My mouth is speaking," but I am speaking. In everyday speech, we do not separate the *I* from the *body*.

Your body, then, according to Merleau-Ponty, is more than a mere machine and is not something separate from a mysterious soul. Rather, it is essential to your identity. Clinical, scientific language has its place in a limited context such as anatomy class or in medicine, but it cannot describe the lived body. Even in medicine, it may not be possible to accurately diagnose all conditions using only tests and scientific language. It may be necessary for a physician to talk to a patient about his or her lived body, about how he or she feels, about the social relationships the patient has in his or her embodied life.

Is Merleau-Ponty correct that your body is more than a machine that can best be described scientifically? Read over both your descriptions again - the clinical description and your description of going to the grocery store. Does your language agree more with Descartes' view of the body or with Merleau-Ponty's? What does your answer say about the nature of your body?

Write Down Your Thoughts, Feelings and Perceptions

Have you ever felt you were of two minds about something, or that thoughts flew by so fast you wondered if you could catch yourself? Set aside fifteen minutes. Get out pen and paper and record every thought, feeling and perception you have during that time. Do not censor yourself. When you are finished, read what you have written. Are there any connections between your thoughts, feelings and perceptions, or did they all seem random? Did you find any evidence of an underlying *self* in your document?

David Hume did not believe in a permanent self or soul. Instead, he accepted the *bundle theory* of the self, according to which the self is a loose collection, or *bundle*, of thoughts, feelings and perceptions without any underlying unity. Is Hume correct? Is your mind just a series of impressions with no real unity or underlying identity? Does your experiment with writing down your thoughts, feelings and perceptions confirm or disconfirm Hume's theory?

René Descartes, a French philosopher often considered to be the founder of modern philosophy, believed that we have a permanent self or soul. He held that we have direct, intuitive knowledge of the existence of our soul when we introspect. That is what you were doing when you were recording your thoughts and feelings - you were *looking inside* your mind and recording what was there. Descartes believed that what you find when you introspect is a unified *thinking thing* which has a wholeness that is more than a mere *bundle of impressions*. Is that what you experienced as you recorded your thoughts, feelings and perceptions? Do you believe Hume or Descartes to be more accurate? Or are they both wrong? Is this exercise an adequate test for whether you have a permanent self or soul? Why or why not?

Reword all Mental Terms as Neurological Terms

A re you feeling anything right now? You might be having feelings of happiness, sadness, pleasure, pain, anger, love or a combination of some of these. Are you thinking about something, perhaps "What kind of silly exercise will this be?" or "I am looking forward to the party this weekend?" We use language about feelings and thoughts all the time -language about what philosophers call *mental contents*. We take for granted that such language is proper. After all, how could we communicate without words such as *love, hate, believe* or *think*?

Is it possible to eliminate all mental terms from our language and replace them with terms referring to neurological processes and secretion of hormones? Try doing it. There is no need to worry if you do not know that much about how the body works; it is fine to "wing it" in this exercise. You are not allowed to use any words referring to thoughts, feelings, or *the self*. Only scientific terminology referring to the brain and bodily processes is permitted.

I will try it myself and give you an example. I will pinch myself until it hurts slightly. Now I must eliminate the word "hurt," since that refers to a mental state, and also eliminate the words "myself" and "*I*." Here is my result: "In brain MP at time 10:52 a.m., C fibers fired in response to stimulation of nerves in right hand pinched by left index fingernail and left thumbnail of body MP."

Now try the same exercise; describe what you are thinking or feeling right now in terms of neurophysiology or in terms of hormones secreted in your body. Do not worry about exact scientific accuracy. Record your results.

Were you able to eliminate all mental terms from your vocabulary and replace them with neurological terms? If so, how difficult was it? Have a friend try to describe his or her thoughts and feelings using only neurological terms. Have your friend try to describe your thoughts and feelings this way. Do you believe our entire language or mental terms could be replaced by such "scientific" terms? Could we communicate with each other using only the language of neurophysiology?

The husband and wife team of Paul (1942-) and Patricia Churchland

(1943-), who teach at the University of California at San Diego, defend a position called *eliminative materialism*. This is the view that eventually all mental terms will be (and should be) totally eliminated from our vocabulary and replaced with the language of neurophysiology. Churchland and Churchland argue that just as language about "thunderbolts from Zeus," referring to lightning, was replaced by the language of electricity, mental language will be replaced by the language of neurons, neurotransmitters, and hormones, given sufficient development of science. Mental terms are part of *folk psychology*, which impedes the progress of science, just as in the past, language about demons and spirits causing diseases impeded the progress of science. Folk psychology will one day go the way of witchcraft and shamanism.

William Lycan (1945-), a philosopher at the University of North Carolina, writes in opposition to Churchland and Churchland. He argues that eliminative materialism is not plausible; the burden of proof is on the eliminative materialist to show that folk psychology is inadequate. Given our extensive use of mental imagery, and how essential it seems to be for our conceptual framework, it is always more plausible, Lycan argues, to accept folk psychological language as proper rather than to eliminate it.

With whom do you agree: Churchland and Churchland or Lycan? Is it really possible to eliminate all mental language from our vocabulary? Will it ever be possible to talk only about neurons, neurotransmitters and hormones rather than about love, joy and anger? How does your experiment affect your answer?

PLAY A GAME OF CHESS WITH A COMPUTER

C an computers think? Chess is considered to be a thinker's game. If you know how to play chess, play a game with a computer. There are a number of inexpensive programs on the market, and you can check the Internet for free chess programs.

Did you win? How did the computer play compared to a human being? If you know chess notation, try this. Have someone who knows how to play chess, with whom you have never played, sit behind a screen. Find a computer program for chess you have never played. Now play four games of chess, two with the human and two with the computer. Have a third person go around the screen to your board and make the moves of either your human or computer opponent. Now guess which opponent was the human being and which was the computer.

Were you right? If not, does this mean that the computer can think in the same way a human being can think?

Alan Turing (1912-1954) developed a test now called *The Turing Test*. The setup is similar to the chess exercise involving a computer and a human being, except that in The Turing Test, the computer carries on a conversation with the person on the other side of the screen. It would not be a spoken conversation, but what today would be called a *chat room* with text messaging. If the person communicating with the computer cannot tell the difference between the computer and an actual human being, Turing suggests the computer can really think. The position that computers can really think is called *strong artificial intelligence* (or *strong AI*).

Do you agree? What about the chess test? If you were unable to determine whether you were playing a computer or a human being, does this mean the computer was thinking when it played chess with you?

John Searle (1932-) taught philosophy for many years at the University of California at Berkeley. He believes that computers can give us some models of human reasoning but themselves are incapable of thought, a position called *weak artificial intelligence* (or *weak AI*). He presented his own thought experiment, *The Chinese Room Experiment*, in which people who do not know Chinese are locked in a room. They are given code which they are told to put together in a particular order. Then they are given more code and are told to respond with code in a particular order according to a set of rules. Unknown to them, someone outside the room who is unaware that the people in the room are being given a list of rules is writing out questions in Chinese. The people inside the room are giving *answers* to the questions based on rules they are given, but they have no idea what the Chinese symbols really mean. Suppose they become so good at following the rules that the man outside reading their answers to questions could not tell the difference between their messages and a native Chinese speaker. This still does not mean the people in the room know Chinese. They are just following a set of formal rules.

Searle argues that computers are the same way - they could be given a set of formal symbols concerning a language, and they could get so good manipulating those symbols that someone could have a conversation with a computer and not be able to tell it's a computer. The computer would still just be following rules and would not really understand a natural language such as English. Nor does it really think when it's playing chess - it is only manipulating formal rules that make no reference to chess.

Does Searle's position make sense? Do you believe that the computer playing you in chess is really gazing at the board in its mind? Is it really thinking chess or is it merely following its programming?

WATCH A MOVIE THAT BRINGS OUT STRONG EMOTION

What is emotion? Is emotion purely irrational, something that happens to a person without that person's choice? Does emotion inevitably involve changes in the body, such as increased heart rate, respiration, or a sinking feeling in the stomach? Or can someone have an emotion without any bodily changes at all?

Watch a movie you have seen before that you know brings out strong emotion in you. Think about the reactions you have after you experience an emotion. Which events in the movie caused you to have an emotional response? Did you notice any physiological changes when you felt an emotion? Did an emotion involve any judgment? For example, suppose you felt fear when a criminal chased a character you liked. Did your feeling involve a judgment that your main character was in danger?

The American philosopher and psychologist William James, along with the psychologist G. C. Lange (1834-1900) developed a theory of the emotions that focused on the bodily changes in emotion. According to their theory, the bodily change comes first and emotion simply is the perception of that feeling (this can also include bodily behavior, such as covering one's eyes or running in the case of fear). They believed, for example, that a person cries first, then feels sad in response to the bodily reaction of crying. Do you agree with their view? Is the meaning of emotion exhausted by perceiving bodily changes? Even if you believe the meaning of emotion involves more than such perception, is bodily change an essential part of emotion? If so, could a disembodied being, such as God or an angel, feel emotion?

Magda Arnold (1903-2002) was an American psychologist. Her theory of emotion focused on cognition. She believed that an emotion, first and foremost, involves an appraisal of a situation. If you see a tiger running toward you, for example, you immediately appraise the tiger as dangerous, and this appraisal is the essential part of the emotion of fear. You then act (run!) based on the initial appraisal of danger. Of course the "fight or flight" bodily response takes place in order that you can run fast and (hopefully) get away from the tiger. The appraisal is more like an intuition than step-by-step reasoning.

Is Arnold correct? When you felt emotion during the movie, did it involve an intuitive judgment that led to you having certain feelings? If a character behaved in a cruel way, did you make a judgment about the cruelty of the action and then feel the emotion, including (perhaps) bodily changes? Alternatively, did the bodily feeling come first and then the judgment? Are James-Lange's theory and Arnold's theory the only options regarding the nature of emotions? If not, what theory would you propose?

RECORD YOUR DREAMS FOR A WEEK

Are your dreams just random firings of neurons in the brain or do they have a deeper meaning? Do your dreams reveal parts of yourself that you would rather hide? Do you ever have dreams that help you in real life?

For a week, record your dreams. It is best to write them down as soon as you wake up, or else you will not remember them. Write quickly and with as much detail as possible. Then consider whether your dreams have any significance for your waking life.

Sigmund Freud (1856-1939), an Austrian, was the founder of psychoanalysis. He believed that dreams revealed those parts of ourselves of which we are not consciously aware, the *unconscious mind*. According to Freud, oftentimes the unconscious mind contains thoughts and feelings we have repressed out of shame. One example is the Oedipus Complex. Freud believed that sexuality is a part of the life of people from an early age. Young boys, he thought, have a desire to kill their fathers and marry their mothers. As they grow older, they cannot accept the guilt of having such feelings, so they suppress them and they become a part of the unconscious. But in dreams, our guard is down, and the desires of the Oedipus Complex may come to the surface. Usually these desires will not be directly seen in a dream, but will appear in symbolic form.

For example, suppose a man dreams of being a piece on a giant chessboard. Let us suppose that he is a rook. He moves across the board and captures the king, who disappears. He then stands in the square next to the queen. Freud might interpret the rook as representing the dreaming man, and the king would represent his father. The rook capturing the king represents the man killing his father. The rook standing in the square next to the queen represents the man marrying his mother.

Do you agree with Freud's view that dreams can reveal important information about our unconscious minds? Even if you disagree with Freud's views on the Oedipus Complex, is Freud correct that dreams reveal important hidden information about ourselves? Did your experiment confirm this position?

Simon Blackburne (1944-), Distinguished Research Professor of

Philosophy at The University of North Carolina, disagrees with Freud. He does not believe that dreams are psychologically significant. Dreams, he believes, are based on the realities we see around us every day. There is no esoteric or symbolic significance to dreams that reveals the thoughts of the unconscious mind. If Blackburne is correct, dreams may remain biologically significant, but they do not help us to better understand ourselves or practically help us live in the waking world.

Do you agree more with Freud or with Blackburne? Does the experience of having recorded your dreams help with your decision? How?

MOVE YOUR ARM

Have you ever thought about how your will tells your body, *Do this,* and you automatically do it? This is something we take for granted. You decide to walk and like magic, your legs respond and you walk. You decide to talk and your lips move, your breath flows through your vocal cords in just the right way, and meaningful sounds called "words" come out. Now move your arm. That seems to be such a simple act, yet it is filled with complexity when we try to explain it. You can try to explain it biologically: a set of neurons fire in the brain, sending a signal to motor neurons in your arm and your muscles contract in response. There is a more important issue - what about your *willing* your arm to move? Is that so simple to explain?

René Descartes proposed an explanation for how you move your arm. Humans are, he thought, composed of two distinct substances, mind and body, which interact. The mind is nonphysical and consists of consciousness, thoughts, will and feelings. The body is physical and is a mechanical object with no thoughts or feelings and is subject to the laws of physics. When you decide to move your arm, it is your mind that makes the decision. The mind interacts with the brain, causing the correct neurons to fire and send their signal to the motor neurons, causing your muscle to contract and your arm to move. Both mind and body are necessary for any purposive movement in the body.

Is Descartes correct? His views seem to be common sense today but is common sense always right? What about scientists and philosophers who believe that there is no mind separate from the brain? What about Descartes' view that changes in the mind cause changes in the body? Can a nonspatial substance cause changes in the physical world?

Arnold Geulincx (1624-1669), a Flemish philosopher, developed an alternative view to Descartes' known as *pre-established harmony*. He believed that the mind cannot cause changes in the body. But God has set up the world such that when you have the thought, *Arm move,* your arm will move. This occurs not because of your mind, but because God has synchronized particular thoughts with particular bodily actions, just as two different clocks can be synchronized to tick at the same time.

Do you agree with Geulincx? Is it true that when you moved your arm, your mind did not cause anything to happen? Is it true that God acts every time you think so that particular thoughts lead to particular actions? Are Descartes' and Geulincx' explanations the only ones available? How would you explain why your arm moves when you have the thought of commanding your arm to move?

THINK ABOUT SOMETHING

When you are thinking, what are you really doing? Are you speaking to yourself? Does thinking necessarily involve using language? Can you think without language?

Think about anything that interests you. Analyze your thinking process. Did it seem as if you were talking to yourself, or did your thinking take another form? If so, what form did it take? Have some friends do the same exercise. How does their experience of thinking compare with yours?

The German philosopher Johann Gottfried Herder (1744-1803) believed that thinking requires the use of language. This is because he identifies thinking with *internal speaking*, a form of *talking to yourself*. If thinking requires such inner speaking, then only beings that use language can think.

Do you agree with Herder? Perform this exercise while thinking about different things. Your friends can do this, too. Does this make a difference? Does thinking seem to be inner speaking, or does anyone have a different view of thinking? Does it matter what subject you are thinking about?

Temple Grandin (1947-) is Professor of Animal Science at Colorado State University. She is also autistic. She says that she could still think before she mastered the use of language since she was *thinking in pictures*. That is, she was thinking through forming a mental image in her mind. Such an image could include visual imagery, but also olfactory (smell), auditory (hearing), gustatory (taste) and tactile (touch) imagery. Her position opens the possibility that nonhuman animals, such as dogs and cats, can think. They do not think in language, but in pictures.

From your own experiment in thinking, do you believe that Grandin is correct? Did you have any experience of *thinking in pictures* apart from language? Now that you have read about Grandin's position, try to think in pictures without using any language. Are you able to do it? Are your friends able to do it? Does this experiment support Herder or Grandin?

Meditate on Your Life

Are you a *self-made person?* This question is not the same as asking if you are rich because of your own hard work. Instead, I am referring to who you are as a person. Did you make yourself from scratch, or did your heredity and environment have anything to do with who you are?

Take a few moments to meditate on your life. Go over every aspect of your character and how it developed over time from childhood on. Did you wholly make yourself or were other forces or other people involved?

Jean-Paul Sartre, a French philosopher who was influential in a philosophical movement known as *existentialism*, believed that we are all *self-made people*. Since, according to Sartre, there is no God, there is no human nature. We have to make our own nature by our free choices. We are, quite literally, *self-creators*. We cannot use our heredity or environment as an excuse for our decisions and character. We cannot use the influences of family, friends, and other people as an excuse. If we claim we are the way we are due to our environment, we are living with *false consciousness*. However, if we make choices and take full responsibility for our decisions, only then do we live an authentic life.

Do you agree with Sartre that your life is made up of your choices and that you must take full responsibility for those choices? Do you agree with him that appeals to other influences, such as heredity, environment or relationships, are mere excuses to avoid responsibility? What was your experience when you meditated on your life?

Burrhus Frederic (B. F.) Skinner (1904-1990) was a psychologist at Harvard University. He believed that our lives are totally determined by our environment. Free will is an illusion. We are not self-made people but we are made by stimulus and response. We receive stimuli from the environment and react in a deterministic way. We do not choose how we respond to our environment.

Do you agree with Skinner that stimuli from our environment and our automatic responses wholly make you who you are today? Was this the sense you had when you did your meditation? Are the only options the views of Sartre and Skinner? Do you have an alternative position to theirs? If so, what is it and how would you defend it?

Philosophy of Religion

Pick up a Rock

Pick up a rock. Is it a piece of limestone from a gravel drive, soft sandstone, granite found beside an abandoned railroad track, or pumice spewed from an ancient volcano? Hold it up to sunlight so you can see every detail. How is it unique? Sure, it may be similar to other rocks, but its patterned surface, exact shape, location - in your hand at this moment - make this rock a one-and-only. That this rock exists at all seems a miracle. How much history had to pass before you were able to hold the rock in your palm?

Let us go back in time to when the rock was chipped from a larger stone. Perhaps it was cut in a quarry. Or maybe water crept between creases, shattering the stone into fragments, one of which became *your* rock. Earlier, the stone may have been part of a mountain, into which wind, rain, and snow carved a crease until the stone split, and fragments fell as new rocks. One of these fell to rest and sank in the earth where it was worn down for thousands of years. Now, go back to an ancient ocean, sediment settling on the floor, weighted down by water. More silt settles, joined by dead plants, corals, shellfish and bony fishes: millennia go by, and limestone is born. Travel further back in time, before life began, and water vapor spews from volcanoes, condenses and falls as rain to fill depressions between fledgling continents, forming the womb of life, the sea. Moving back even more, you find the molten earth - and no atmosphere. Lava glows bright yellow and flows before solidifying into stone. A rain of meteorites strikes the new stone, heating it until it is molten again - and the cycle repeats.

Now take your journey through time and space to debris from a supernova explosion, hydrogen floating free in space along with heavy elements: oxygen, carbon, iron. These congeal into a cloud of dust and gas which condenses into the sun, Mercury, Venus, Earth, the other planets. Earlier, a large blue star burns out fast before exploding into stardust. By then galaxies had already formed. Before they formed, you find only intense light and heat. As you come closer to the beginning of time, you discover darkness, condensed matter and energy. Finally, you reach the beginning, when a lone singularity, a mathematical point, about which we can say very little, explodes in a big bang.

All this had to occur to create the rock you are grasping in your hand right now. If one step were missing, this rock would not exist. The rock does not *have* to exist - but it does, because a thread of causes and effects keeps it outside of nothingness.

What will you do with this rock? Will you drop it, keep it on your bookcase or desk, or crush it into dust? Remember, though, all that had to happen for your rock to exist. Ponder these questions: Is the rock really a unique individual? What about the minerals that compose it or the grains that hold it together? Could there be a rock exactly like yours in every way?

Imagine yourself using a hammer and chisel to break the rock into two or more parts. Have you now become a god, creating multiple individuals from one?

The rock you are holding does not have to be; there is no necessity for it to exist (that is, its existence is *contingent*). It is possible for your rock to exist or not to exist. You know this because you realize that there was a time in the past during which the rock did not exist. Most likely, there will be a time in the future when it is worn down into dust, or geological forces change its chemical composition. Is this contingency something trivial or significant? In his third way to prove the existence of God, St. Thomas Aquinas argues that the existence of even *one* contingent being implies that a necessary being, that is, a being that *has* to exist (that is, *God*) must exist. Do you think that the existence of your rock proves the existence of God? Why or why not?

WATCH PEOPLE FROM ABOVE

Have you ever looked down at people from heights? Maybe you were on an airplane and watched people on the ground shrink into dots as the plane ascended. Perhaps you looked down from an observation tower. Find a tall place from which you can observe people. It might be a room in a tall building, or a hill near your home. As you watch people walk below, can you see what they are doing and where they are going?

For example, suppose you are looking down from an observation tower and see the visitor's center at a park. A crowd of children led by an adult walks towards the door. The adult holds the door open and the children begin to file in. The teacher chooses to open the door. The children choose to walk inside. Does your seeing the adult and children walk in the building in any way determine what happens? In your own experience of looking down at people from a higher point, did your knowledge of people's actions take away their free will to do what they desired?

Traditional Jews, Christians, and Moslems believe that God knows our future actions. With God, it is not merely a matter of predicting our future actions - God *knows* for certain what we will do in the future. Nelson Pike (1930-2010), who taught philosophy at the University of California at Irvine, holds that if God knows what we will do in the future, we are bound by necessity and lack free will. Free will involves, he states, the power to do otherwise. For example, if you decide to eat an apple, you had the free will to decide to eat an orange or grapefruit. But if God knows you are going to eat an apple, then how could you do otherwise? Since God's knowing you will eat an apple means you cannot do otherwise than eating an apple, God's knowledge of your future choices takes away your free will, and you are bound by necessity.

Do you agree with Pike? What about your action of peering down at people from above? Were you really in a *godlike* position to know what they would do, or did you only know what they were doing in the present? Was your standpoint on a hill really a good analogy to God's knowledge of people?

St. Thomas Aquinas believes that God's knowledge of our future choices does not take away our free will. He argues that God is eternal; that is, He is outside of time. Every event to God is present, not past or future. Thus, a moment ten million years in the past is, from God's point of view, the present moment. A moment a day in the future or a billion years in the future are both present moments to God, not future ones. Now when you were on the hill or on top of a building looking down, you could make predictions of people's futures, but that is not like God's knowledge. What is like God's knowledge is when you watch people's present actions. So if you see someone walk into a building, such seeing does not make the person walk into a building. In a similar way, if God sees you eat an apple on January 25 ten years from now at 11 a.m., he does not see it as future, but as *now*. That no more takes away your free choice than you watching people's actions from a standpoint above them takes away their free choice.

Do you agree with Aquinas? Does it make sense to say that all times are *present* to God? Does the analogy between God's knowledge and your knowledge when you were up high work?

DIG A HOLE FOR NO REASON

If you have a lawn on land you own, or a garden on land you rent, dig a
hole. If you do not have land to which you have access, fill a cup with
dirt and dig a hole. Do this for no reason (other than digging a hole
being part of this exercise). Fill up the hole. Then dig it again. Repeat as
many times as you can.

Does the exercise seem pointless? Were you bored? What if life were
like that? Would that imply that there is no meaning to life?

The French writer George Bataille (1897-1962) believed that God
does not exist. He also, like Buddhists and the British philosopher David
Hume, did not believe in any permanent self or soul. A world without
God, he believed, is meaningless, without value. He believed that life is
just wasted energy, *expenditure* with no purpose. To him, life really is no
different than digging and filling a hole for no reason.

Do you agree with Bataille? Does your life ever feel like the process
you went through in digging and filling a hole - using up energy on
various projects that have no real purpose - or do you believe there is real
meaning in life, either through God or some other source of meaning? Is
Bataille correct to believe that atheism implies that life is without
meaning?

Another French philosopher, Albert Camus, agreed with Bataille's
atheism. He also agreed that in a world without God, there could be no
objective meaning to life. That is, there is no meaning to life that can be
found in the nature of reality outside our own minds. However, he
disagreed with Bataille that life is just a wasting of energy with no purpose
at all. There is still room for *subjective* meaning, meaning that a person can
find within that person's self.

In a famous essay, *The Myth of Sisyphus*, Camus refers to the ancient
Greeks' story of Sisyphus, a man who offended the gods. As punishment,
he had to push a rock up a hill. Just as the rock reached the top of the
hill, it rolled down, and Sisyphus had to push it up again. He repeated this
process forever.

Pushing a rock up a hill that falls down seems just as pointless as
digging a hole and filling it. In fact, Camus goes to the point of saying the
only meaningful question in philosophy is whether or not one should

commit suicide. Camus, thankfully, does not believe that suicide is the right option. He believes that Sisyphus can be happy if he finds his own personal meaning in pushing the rock. In the same way, although life may be objectively pointless, we can make our own personal meanings and find happiness. We should embrace our projects in life and find meaning in them, whether that involves pushing a rock up a hill or being successful in business. When we *do our own thing* and embrace that thing that we are doing as our purpose in life, we are not wasting our energy.

Do you agree with Camus that without God, there is no objective meaning to life? Do you agree with him that even if there is no objective meaning in life, you can find your own personal meaning in whatever you do? Look back to your experience of digging and filling a hole. Could you embrace that project and give it meaning, perhaps coming to enjoy it? Or is it merely a meaningless waste of energy?

List the Things You Would Want to Do
if You Lived Forever

Have you ever wondered if you will continue to exist after death? You may believe that you are annihilated at death, or you might believe you are reincarnated or live as a disembodied soul after death. Perhaps you believe your body will be raised as a perfect, immortal body. Whatever you believe about life after death, pretend that you will live after death as the same person you are now. Then list everything you would like to do if you lived forever. The list could include places you would like to see, including places on earth - but also other planets, stars or galaxies. There might be hobbies you would like to take up or game skills you wish to perfect. If you play football, you might want to play with the best players in football history - with Red Grange, Roger Staubach or Peyton Manning. If you play golf, you might want to play with Bobby Jones, Arnold Palmer, Jack Nicklaus or Tiger Woods.

If you are more intellectual, you might want to read all the great works of literature ever written. If you enjoy writing, you could perfect your writing skills and write a great novel or a book of beautiful poems. If you are a scientist, you would have eternity to discover the secrets of the atom or of living things. If you are religious, you might desire to know more about God and to get to know God better. Perhaps you would like to deepen friendships with family members and friends as well. Make the list as long as you would like. Have your friends come up with their own lists and compare yours to theirs.

Bernard Williams (1929-2003), a British philosopher who taught at Cambridge, Oxford, and The University of California at Berkeley, believed that eternal life would eventually become worse than death. He thought that no matter how many things we wish to do, eventually eternal life would become boring. We would run out of things to do that interest us, and over time, we would reach the point that we would desire death rather than continued existence.

Do you agree with Williams? Look over your list again. Discuss this issue with your friends, who will have their own list. Do you agree that eternal life would be boring?

Thomas Aquinas did not believe eternal life would be boring.

Aquinas believed that after death, those who are saved from sin will enjoy the *beatific vision* of God. That is, they will know God as He really is, and will also be able to see Jesus (Aquinas was a Catholic Christian) with their own eyes. Since God is the source of all good things, people will never run out of activities and people to interest them. And for Aquinas, God is the most interesting person of all, since He is infinite goodness.

Do you agree with Aquinas that the vision of God would make everything after death more interesting? Do you agree with him that such a life would never be boring? Or is Williams's position the better one? Do you have an alternative understanding of eternal life? If so, what is it?

What is a *Dkayems*?

When you read a word you cannot identify, what do you do? Perhaps you go to a good dictionary, and if you do not find the meaning there, you *google* it. If I were to tell you a word and ask you to identify what it refers to, you would probably take these routes, or else I could give you clues to help you along.

What is a *Dkayems*? Try to find it in a dictionary and on the Internet. If you fail to find it, one way I can give you clues is by telling you that the word is a noun - that means it must refer to a person, place or thing. What kind of thing?

I continue by telling you what it is not: It is not a bird. It is not a table. It is not a newspaper. How much information does that give you? Can you identify what a *Dkayems* is now? If not, do you have at least some minimal information about the reference of the word that you did not have before?

What if I told you that a *Dkayems* is beyond even negative description? I cannot describe it in either terms of what it is or in terms of what it is not. In fact, I am unable to describe it at all. Are you feeling frustrated? If so, what is the source of that frustration?

To whom or what does the word, *God*, refer? In the great monotheistic religions of Judaism, Christianity and Islam, philosophers and theologians have debated about how to refer to God. Augustine, Bishop of Hippo in North Africa, believed we could know who God is negatively, by saying what God is not. God is *not finite, without any evil or flaw*, etc. While this does not give us any positive knowledge of God, it does give us real information since it tells us what God is not.

Abu Sulaiyman Muhammed al-Sijistani (c. 950 A.D.) was a Muslim philosopher who lived in Baghdad. He emphasized the *radical transcendence* of God - that is, God is totally separate and beyond His creation. We cannot describe God positively or negatively; we cannot describe God, period. But if we are unable to describe God at all, are we in any different position concerning God than we are concerning *Dkaymas*? Does al-Sijistani's position imply that the word, *God*, is a nonsense term, or does it properly emphasize the transcendence of God? Do you see any inconsistencies in al-Sijistani's position?

Does Augustine help us any more than al-Sijistani's? How much can I really know if I only have negative knowledge of God? If I tell you that *Dkaymas* is *not an animal or plant*, does this say what *Dkaymas* is? Would it make any difference to your answer if I informed you that *Dkaymas* is a nonsense word I made up?

HOLD A $20 BILL IN YOUR HAND

Have you ever wished for something you didn't have and later got your wish? Was it better to be holding the thing you wished for than to be thinking about it? Does something really existing make it better?

Take a $20.00 bill out of your wallet or purse. Hold it in your hand. What is good about the $20.00 bill? If you took it to a store, could you spend it?

Now think about a $20.00 bill. What makes it a $20.00 bill rather than a one or five? If you went to the store with the thought of a $20.00 bill, could you spend that thought? Do you think you could convince the store manager that the thought of a $20.00 bill is really worth $20.00?

Anselm was Archbishop of Canterbury in England. He developed an interesting argument for the existence of God called the *Ontological Argument*. In it, he argues that since to exist is better than not to exist, a most perfect being has to really exist rather than exist only in your mind. If the most perfect being only exists in your mind, the most perfect being is not the most perfect being. That is like saying an apple is not an apple or a dog is not a dog - it is a contradiction. Since contradictions cannot be true, the most perfect being must really exist. Since the most perfect being is God, God must exist.

What do you think about this argument? In particular, what do you think about Anselm's belief that it is better to exist than not to exist? How does your experience with the $20.00 bill influence your answer?

The great German philosopher Immanuel Kant disagreed with Anselm's belief that existence makes something better. He argued that existence does not add anything to the concept of something. That is, you define a $20.00 bill the same way whether $20.00 bills exist or not. If the government confiscated all $20.00 bills and refused to make any more, you would still define a $20.00 bill in the same way. Existence is not a property in the same way as *having the value of $20.00* is a property of $20.00 bills.

Do you agree with Kant? If he is right that existence

does not make a concept any better, is it true that existence does not make something better in any sense?

PHILOSOPHY OF SCIENCE

IMAGINE WALKING ON MARS

Your spaceship has safely landed on Mars. Tired after a trip of nearly a year, you are ready to disembark. Looking out the porthole at the red, dusty soil, igneous rocks, distant dunes of sand and the daytime sky with its scattered light, it might be tempting to open the spacecraft door without your space suit. You think better of it, knowing that death would come quickly from a thin atmosphere consisting primarily of carbon dioxide. So you get dressed, open the hatch and take the first tentative steps to touch the surface with your booted feet. What is the nature of your experience?

Is there something familiar about Mars? Does it remind you of a desert on earth, perhaps the colorful deserts of Arizona and Utah? Do the rocks remind you of volcanic rocks on earth, the duned hills of the Sahara? In the sky, you notice thin, wispy clouds, which look like earth's cirrus clouds. Perhaps you could feel at home here. Sure, settlers would have to build a pressurized shelter with sufficient oxygen for life, as well as protection from ultraviolet radiation, and a good heating system to keep out the Antarctic cold of Mars that chills even in summer. They would have to set up a greenhouse to grow vegetables. Over time, the settlers could get used to this and eventually bear children, the first generation of human beings not born on earth.

You may, however, have the opposite reaction to being on another world - you feel disconcerted, out of place. Does Mars seem more alien than homelike, a cold, barren wasteland? On Earth's deserts you can breathe, and most of them are hot rather than bitter cold - not so on Mars. The red tinge of the Martian sky may appear alien, a bloody tinge painted over the daytime sky replacing earth's familiar blue. When you look outside your spacecraft at night, you notice a starlike speck, the earth from which you came. Instead of feeling at home, you may feel isolated, as if neither you nor other human beings belong here.

Is there a third option? Do you feel as if you are *both* in a familiar landscape *and* on an alien world? Do you feel at home and lost at the same time? You interpret what you see on Mars in light of what you know, your own world - and you find similarities, but there are so many differences. Are these feelings - of familiarity yet strangeness -

contradictory or complementary?

Now return to earth, to your own home. Go outside and stand on a familiar landscape - perhaps your back yard - in twilight, as more and more stars shine through growing darkness. Does your back yard seem familiar? Turn around and watch the horizon. Imagine the surface on which you're walking as part of the sphere of the earth in space. As you look above the horizon, imagine stars flying through the expanse of space, including our own sun hiding underneath the horizon. Focus now on the earth's rotation, the solar system soaring through space, the Milky Way speeding in the expansion of the universe. Imagine the earth as it appeared to the astronauts when they viewed it from the moon. Does the earth seem less familiar now? Does it seem like just another small planet, like Mars, orbiting an average-sized star in a vast galaxy among millions of other galaxies? Does the earth still feel like home? Or does it now feel totally alien. Or a mixture of both?

Even if it felt earthlike, you knew when you were *on* Mars that it was another world, one planet among others. But if you felt that way when on earth, in your own backyard, how could you account for this feeling? When Galileo (1564-1642) supported the theory of Copernicus (1473-1543), which placed the sun at the center of the solar system, this disturbed some people, for they felt as if the earth was less special. Is the earth really less special? Does the fact that the earth is one planet among others somehow make it less important? Does it make the earth seem more like our special home or more of a stranger to us? Does the fact that our bodies are adapted to the earth environment rather than to the Mars environment make any difference in your answer?

RIDE AN ELEVATOR

The next time you are in a building with an elevator, take a ride to the top. Do you feel as if you are being pushed down to the elevator floor as you accelerate and ascend? Do you feel heavier? You may have experienced similar feelings when you accelerate in your car, feeling as if you are being pushed back into your seat. What happens when you accelerate at a constant rate? Do you feel any differently than when you accelerate at an uneven rate of speed?

Can you tell the difference between acceleration and gravity? Both seem to be forces that push against you in some way. It seems, however, that ascending an elevator or driving a car does not tell us about gravity. Didn't Isaac Newton (1643-1727) say that gravity was a force that is proportional to a body's mass? Yet it is as near to you as your landing on our feet after you jump into the air. So what, if anything, does gravity have to do with acceleration?

Quite a bit, according to Albert Einstein (1879-1955). In his general theory of relativity, Einstein affirmed that gravity and acceleration are equivalent. You cannot really tell, for example, when you are accelerating at a constant rate, whether you are feeling the force of gravity or the force of acceleration.

The point of this science lesson is to encourage you to think about the point of doing science. So what if gravity and acceleration are equivalent? Newton did not consider that option, but his equations are sufficient for making calculations regarding, for example, the trajectories of space vehicles that travel to planets such as Mars. At a practical level, Newton's theory of gravitation seems to be just as good as Einstein's. Was Einstein, then, wasting his time when he developed his theory of gravitation?

One popular view of science in the modern period was developed by the English philosopher Francis Bacon (1561-1626). Bacon believed that the purpose of science is to question nature, wringing out answers useful for improving human life. He even uses the image of someone being stretched on a rack: nature itself must be *placed on the rack* to give up its secrets. Once this occurs, technology can use such secrets to build a better world - at least for human beings. He does not consider the impact on other animals, plants or the environment.

Is Bacon's view of science correct? If you agree with his view of the proper motivation for doing science, it does appear that Einstein might have been wasting his time when he came up with his theory of gravitation. Now someone might argue that there may be technological benefits that can be gained from his theory, but we are not aware of them yet. But suppose there are none - and Newton's theory of gravitation is the only one we need to make calculations useful for space flight and other technological applications. It seems as if it really would not matter whether you are experiencing gravity or the effects of acceleration in the elevator. Do you think that is what follows from Bacon's view of science? Is lessening human misery and furthering human happiness the only reasons one can cite for pursuing science? As long as the technology works and does not harm you, what difference does it make what is really going on while you are riding the elevator or driving your car? If the scientific theory works at a practical level, why care about anything else?

Still, do you ever wonder what is really going on while you are riding an elevator? Sure, you realize that it may not make a big difference for elevator technology or how you feel while ascending. Despite this fact, have you ever felt a sense of dissatisfaction in not knowing how the world really is? Aristotle said that *philosophy begins in wonder*. Might this be the case with science as well? Could it be a good thing that there are people who wonder what makes the world tick, who continue to search for better ways to understand it, including understanding gravitation better? Would Einstein have ceased to do physics if he had believed there would be no technological benefits from his discoveries? Could science be pursued as having value in itself, even if it turns out to be without practical benefits? If humans are naturally curious about reality, might they continue to seek knowledge about gravity and other phenomena, despite current theories working well?

Think back to your elevator ride. Are you asking, "Who cares whether Einstein or Newton are right; the elevator works just fine either way?" Or are you now wondering what gravity really is, whether it really is the same as acceleration? Has the search for knowledge, just for the sake of knowledge, begun to become part of who you are?

TURN ON A FAUCET

Have you ever wondered why the weather is so hard to predict? Do you remember a time you had plans and the weather forecast predicted sunny weather and rain poured down? Are there aspects of nature that cannot be predicted? If there are, are they unpredictable in themselves or only because of our lack of knowledge?

Turn on a faucet in your home. Start out with the water flowing smoothly. Then turn the faucet close to *off* but only with enough force for there to be a slow, regular drip. Can you determine when the next drop will fall? Are you correct? Now turn the faucet up just a little, until the drops start falling irregularly. Can you predict when the next drop will fall? Turn the faucet up as high as it will go and watch droplets of water as they spray from the stream. Can you see any pattern in those droplets or does it seem random?

Most likely, you were unable to predict when the next drop would fall in the irregular dripping. You probably were unable to detect a pattern in the drops slinging off when the faucet was turned on full. You might think a scientist could make such predictions, but this is not the case, not even with the help of supercomputers. Why is this the case?

Chaos theory involves laws that seem to be predictable mathematically, but practically speaking, we cannot make accurate predictions except for some short term predictions, such as the five-day weather forecast. This is because of *sensitive dependence on initial conditions*. You may have heard about the term, *the butterfly effect*. This is usually illustrated with the idea is that a butterfly flapping its wings in Peru could cause a hurricane to develop off the coast of Africa. In chaotic systems, tiny changes can have huge effects. That is why it is impossible to predict the weather with 100% accuracy, even though forecasters can make fairly accurate predictions up to a five day range. Tiny changes in the atmosphere can have big effects on weather patterns.

When you turned on the water at a high enough speed to produce irregular dripping, tiny changes based on the number of particles in the water, the texture of the faucet as the water flows through it, the dust particles in the air when the drops fall - all these affect the time when the next drop will come. The same problems arise with the tiny droplets sloughed off when you turned the faucet on high. The issue for the philosopher is this: does this mean that nature has an element that is not determined totally by scientific laws?

Ilya Prigogine (1917-2003), a Belgian physicist and chemist, believed that chaos theory implies that nature itself is indeterministic. That is, he believes that chaos theory shows that there is *metaphysical indeterminism* in nature, indeterminism that operates in reality apart from our knowledge. This implies that not knowing when the next drop will fall is not because of your lack of knowledge, but due to nature itself having an element of unpredictability. Does this make sense to you? If nature is unpredictable, does this imply that scientific law no longer operates, or that scientific laws have exceptions?

Stephen H. Kellert (1963-), Professor of Philosophy at Hamline University in St. Paul, Minnesota, disagrees with Prigogine. He believes that the determinism in chaotic systems is *epistemological* rather than metaphysical. That is, due to our lack of knowledge, our inability to calculate all the tiny factors that can cause big changes in chaotic systems, they are unpredictable. But since the mathematical equations of chaos are deterministic, the systems are *metaphysically* deterministic. Do you think that part or all of our inability to predict chaotic systems is due to our lack of knowledge rather than due to nature itself being unpredictable? What do you think given your experience with the faucet? Are there any implications of your answer for questions such as whether human beings have free will?

DRAW A TRIANGLE ON A BALL

Have you ever studied geometry? Even if you have not taken a course in geometry, you probably covered formulas about various shapes during your time in school. Was it frustrating to you that in math courses such as geometry, there was only one right answer, or was this a comfort to you? You may be aware that in a triangle, the sum of the interior angles is equal to 180 degrees. Architects and engineers have used the exact answers of geometry since the pyramids of Egypt to plan their buildings. The laws of geometry appear to be universal and necessary, and questioning them seems to be a mark of irrationality.

Find a spherical ball such as a beach ball, one large enough on which you can draw a triangle. Draw the lines as "straight" as you can, being aware that you have no choice but to follow the curvature of the ball. Use a protractor to measure the interior angles of the triangle. What is the sum? Does the answer surprise you?

Immanuel Kant was impressed by the system of geometry developed by the Greek mathematician Euclid, who lived and worked around 300 B.C. Euclid's geometry was based on "flat" space, in which parallel lines never meet, and in which the sum of the interior angles of a triangle always equal 180 degrees. He began with certain assumptions he took for granted, called *axioms*. From these axioms, he proved *theorems*, and from a combination of these he proved other theorems. The structure was logical, and if one accepts Euclid's initial axioms, invulnerable to attack. Kant believed that Euclid's geometry was a necessary and universal structure in the human mind, essential for us to have experience of the world. Is Kant correct? Does the geometry you learned seem necessary and universal? Is it an essential part of the way you experience the world? Does the experiment with drawing a triangle on a sphere affect your answer?

Bernhard Riemann (1826-1866), a German mathematician, developed an alternate system of geometry based on (to oversimplify) spherical space rather than flat space. In this space, the sum of the interior angles of a triangle equals more than 180 degrees. His geometry is one version of a *non-Euclidean geometry*, one that departs from Euclid's version of geometry. Do you believe that the development of non-Euclidean geometries, such as Riemann's, means that Euclid's system is not universal and necessary (as Kant believed) for experience of the world? Does your experiment with the ball affect your answer, especially given that the earth is a sphere? Can Kant modify his position so as to allow the possibility of non-Euclidean geometries? If so, how?

Try to Reverse Time

Why does time never seem to go backwards? Is there anything in the nature of the world that makes time going forward necessary? Why can't spilled milk return to its glass? Why doesn't someone grow younger rather than grow older?

Try to reverse time. Drop a baseball and wait for it to rise back to your hand the same way it arrived. Do you think if that happened you would know you dropped the ball? Why or why not? Run down the street. Do you return backwards to your original place and time? Maybe time keeps moving backwards and you reach the time before you read this exercise. Again, if you did, would you realize that time went backwards? Is it possible that time moves backwards quite often and that no one is aware of it?

Albert Einstein is famous for his theory of relativity. Most of us are probably familiar with the implication of the theory that the faster you go, the slower time goes. But you may not be familiar with the fact that the mathematical equations of relativity theory work just as well if time goes backwards. There is no barrier in the theory of relativity to time traveling either forward or backwards. Does this change your position on whether time could go backwards? Were the results of your experiment conclusive to you in showing the direction of time?

Ilya Prigogine, a Belgian scientist, believed that time moves forward because of the phenomena of entropy. Entropy refers to the fact that usable energy tends to become dispersed over time. For example, if you boil water, the heat energy is slowly dispersed until the water is the same temperature as the surrounding room. Sometimes the principle is expressed in terms of things moving from order to disorder. We can see this principle in an everyday example. If you fail to clean your room for a long time, what happens? Does the room become more orderly? Most likely it does not. These processes go one direction. When you break a glass, it does not come together again. Water does not boil on its own. Prigogine believed that since these processes are unidirectional, time must be unidirectional as well. Although there is a slight statistical chance that the ball you threw down could return to your hand - it is not impossible for time to flow backwards - the chances of this occurring are so slim as to be practically nonexistent.

Do you agree with Prigogine? Can your experiment disprove Prigogine's or Einstein's position? Why or why not?

Play with a Magnet

As a child, did you ever play with magnets? Did you find the magnetic force mysterious? Find two magnets at home or buy cheap ones at a store. Then find some small objects made of iron or steel, such as nails or tacks. Does the magnet have to touch the objects to attract them? Does this seem strange - an invisible force pulling something from which it is separated in space to itself? Now try putting the magnets close together. If they join together, try turning one to the opposite end. What happens? You probably remember from elementary science that two ends of the same charge (two positive or two negatives) will repel each other and those with different charges attract. But does knowing the science keep this force from being any less mysterious?

Modern science had trouble dealing with forces such as magnetism (and gravitation) because it seemed that they involved action at a distance - objects not in contact with others causing changes in other objects. An example of this line of thought is found in the great French philosopher René Descartes. Descartes did not like the idea of action at a distance. He believed it reeked of occult and mysterious forces he thought were in Aristotle's science. Modern science must avoid anything that hints of superstition, and to Descartes, action at a distance was superstition. Thus, he did not believe in empty space. He thought that the universe is a *plenum*, filled with extended objects that impart motion by touch. Forces such as magnetism and gravity must be explained in terms of objects touching one another rather than by action at a distance.

Do you agree with Descartes? Do you believe that action at a distance implies occult forces? Do you believe that there must be some kind of contact, even if you cannot see all the objects involved, for a magnet to work?

The French mathematician and scientist Charles Augustin de Coulomb (1736-1806) understood magnetism in terms of action at a distance. Although later physicists worked in this framework, many scientists felt uncomfortable with action at a distance, and eventually James Clerk Maxwell (1831-1879) developed a theory unifying electricity and magnetism and understanding them as waves traveling through space. This eliminated action at a distance. But what if Coulomb had been right?

Suppose the magnets in your experiment were really acting at a distance on other objects and on each other. Would this disturb you? Can science still operate if it accepts action at a distance? Why or why not?

Epistemology

TASTE AN ORANGE BEFORE AND AFTER
EATING CHOCOLATE

Take a bite of a juicy navel orange (if you dislike oranges find another fruit such as an apple or pear). Savor the sweet-tart taste. Now eat something sugary, such as a chocolate candy bar. Bite the fruit again. What is the flavor now?

Did you notice the taste is different, that what was once sweet-tart is now almost too sour to bear? How can this be? Isn't it true that when oranges are ripe, they are tangy-sweet? What happened to the sweetness? Was the flavor in the orange itself and then somehow left the orange? But the orange did not change just because you ate a piece of chocolate. It remains the same fruit you took a bite out of a few moments ago.

Perhaps the taste is not in the fruit at all but only in your mind. Yet if the taste is only in your mind, why did you taste the orange only when you took a bite out of it? If flavors are only in your mind, would it be possible for you to experience them when you are not eating or drinking?

Perhaps the sweet flavor is *both* in the orange *and* in your mind. But then which part of the flavor is in the orange and which part is in your mind? How can the orange have the flavor in itself, since a flavor is by definition something a person *tastes*? Taste implies awareness, consciousness - are we willing to entertain the possibility that an orange is conscious?

There is another possibility. Perhaps the orange has a particular molecular structure. When you bite into the orange, the molecules in the orange cause changes in the taste buds in your tongue. That information is transmitted by nerves to the brain, where the flavor in the orange is interpreted as sweet and/or sour. When you eat the chocolate, its molecular structure also affects the taste buds, and the brain interprets the information as a sweet flavor. The changes in the taste buds caused by the sweet chocolate interact with the second attempt at eating the orange; as a result, the orange now tastes totally sour. It is similar to the effect of putting one's hand in ice water, then putting it into lukewarm water - the lukewarm water seems to be hot. What is *in* the orange is its molecular structure, not the flavor - at least according to a view similar to John Locke's.

He made a distinction between primary and secondary qualities. For Locke, a quality is the ability of a material object to produce an idea (sensation or thought) in the mind. Primary qualities are measurable qualities such as size, shape and solidity. These qualities *represent* what is really in the material object. In the case of the orange, it literally has its roundish-oval shape, its mass and its texture. But secondary qualities do not represent what is literally in the object - they are caused by the interaction of the primary qualities in the object with your sense receptors (eyes, nose, ears, taste buds on the tongue) and your brain. The molecular structure (primary quality) of the orange interacts with our taste buds and brain, and our brain interprets the interaction as *sweet-tartness* or, after we eat the chocolate, just *tartness*.

But if this account is true, what do we mean when we say, *Oranges are sweet*? Is this a lie? And if flavors are not in food, what of colors in flowers or sounds in waterfalls? Much of what we appreciate in the world seems to be dependent on us rather than being literally in the world.

So, where *is* the flavor of the orange - in the orange or in you?

Step into a Puddle

I magine that you are a child again after a fresh rain. You run outside in bare feet, find a puddle of clear water. You reach down and touch the surface, which bends like liquid glass. You see a mosquito or two dancing like ice skaters on the top, watch them while trying to avoid their bites. You can clearly see green grass underwater. A few blades poke through the surface; the parts below the water's surface seem shifted from those above. You realize that this is an optical illusion, yet how do you know for sure where the blade of grass really is? You are conditioned to think that the position of the part poking above the water is the actual one. Would a creature living underwater, looking up toward the surface, come to the same conclusion? How reliable are our senses? Do we require more than sense experience alone to tell us what is real and what is illusion? René Descartes believed that if we would doubt everything possible to doubt, we would find a firm foundation on which to build all other knowledge. He said that we take sensory experience as being truthful - but do we know that is the case? Do we know, without a doubt, the *true* appearance of the grass in the water?

Continuing to look down, you notice the reflections of trees, clouds and bits of blue sky, mirrored so much you wonder if you are watching some parallel universe. Is our own universe as real as some reflection in a pool of water? You might imagine stepping into the puddle as if it were some other world, as in C. S. Lewis's *The Magician's Nephew* from his *Chronicles of Narnia*. Dip your fingers in the pool; feel them go from warm and dry to cool and wet. Stand up and splash your feet in the puddle, and feel the flying drops strike your legs. Notice the swirls of mud forming and flowing around each foot, growing in size as they spread and coalesce. Can you predict exactly where the swirls will move? Do you know when a new sub-swirl will form and how it will move? Suppose the smallest movement of your toe will change the patterns completely so that you cannot possibly predict the appearance or exact movement of the swirls. Would this unpredictability add to your enjoyment of the experience? Perhaps it does not matter, and you find peace watching with fascination the eddy's shape-shifting patterns until the pool turns from clear to brown. It is now opaque, and you can no longer see the blades of grass covered by the water.

You step out of the water and wait. It does not clear; you know mud specks must be floating down to the bottom to rest between grass blades and clover. Is the puddle now ruined? If you leave it alone, will it return to its former state? Will it be as clear as it was before, mirroring the sky and trees like a photograph? Will it be a mud hole until the water finally evaporates? Since you know the water will evaporate, does it really matter that you marred its clarity? It is going to disappear soon, to be replaced by others in the next hard rain.

Perhaps what matters to you is not our little intellectual dance, but the joy of playing in a puddle again, a return, for a moment, to childhood. For a short time, you had fun stepping in a puddle - finding joy in something just because it exists.

Seeing the Expected

Is what you see what you get? If something looks like a chicken, clucks like a chicken, and eats corn scattered by the farmer, must it be a chicken? It seems that sight is the most reliable of our senses. We see things as they really are. If I see the moon, I know exactly what it is as soon as I see it.

Is sight really this simple? Do our expectations ever influence what we see? You may remember staring through the eyepiece of a microscope in biology lab, trying to find a mitochondrion in a muscle cell. At first the cell appears as some vague blob with light and dark spots within a blurry membrane. You might need the teacher's help to discover any identifiable structures. When the teacher shows you the mitochondrion, you may still fail to see it - or, you may have a moment of enlightenment when you see it. The interior of the cell makes sudden sense. Once you were trained to expect to see something, you *saw* it. But if that's the case, what is *really* out there to see?

Imagine you're a physician and scientist living in late fifteenth century Europe. Although dissections of human bodies are rare, autopsies are permitted for deaths in suspicious circumstances. A young man lies dead on a stone table; rumor says he was poisoned. You do not cut the body; that is the barber's job. As he slices the torso, you fail to find an obvious cause of death. Yet you see the familiar organs and mouth to yourself their names and functions, just as you read in the books of the great Roman physician Galen. The liver, the large organ, makes blood. The lungs take in air and expel fiery vapors. Blood ebbs and flows through veins like the tides. You recognize that the liver never rests in its task of making blood, since there is no circuit of blood through the body. You spot the silent heart that once expanded like a bellows, sucking in blood from the veins, banging against the chest wall with every beat. Your eyes focus on the septum that divides the left from the right side of the heart. Moving closer, you find the pores through which blood flows through the septum from one side to the other. You are astonished at the order you see, every part serving a purpose contributing to the good of the whole.

At this point you might snap out of your vision of the past and say,

"Now wait a minute. This isn't what I learned in science class. The liver does not make blood but is the chemical factory of the body. The blood does not ebb and flow in the veins, but returns to the heart, from where it is pumped to the lungs to be oxygenated. Then it returns to the left side of the heart, from where it is pumped out to the arteries to nourish the body. The blood circulates. The heart is a pump; its active motion is when it contracts to pump out blood; when it is expanded, it is relaxed. Those people who lived in the ancient world and in the Middle Ages had it backwards. After all, there is no hole in the septum of the heart in a normal heart. How could anyone *see* such things? This *scientist* must have been imagining it all."

Yet what if you had never heard the modern theory of the liver or of the blood's circulation? The circulation of the blood was a recent discovery; due to the work of the English physician William Harvey (1578-1657). If you had lived before that time, would you have seen the same liver, heart and blood vessels as those who lived after Harvey? If you were a physician living in Europe, you would have most likely accepted the positions of the Roman physician Galen (c. 130-220). Is this any different than accepting your biology textbook's interpretation of cellular structure? Don't you identify the structures your book and your teacher say you ought to identify?

Had you lived in 1500 and saw a heart in a dissected body, what would you have seen? A pump? Holes in the septum? If you saw a liver, would you see a chemical factory and filter, or a blood-maker? In the first edition of his great work on human anatomy, *On the Fabric of the Human Body*, Vesalius (1514-1564) said he saw pores in the septum of the heart. Later, he could not find pores, but expressed gratitude for the existence of invisible pores. Finally, he affirmed that there are no pores. Was he deluded at first, or was he seeing what he expected to see? Were his *observations* of the heart, to some extent, dependent on Galen's *theory* of the heart? How much, then, is your own sight theory-dependent?

TIE YOUR SHOES USING A LIST OF RULES

If you are like me, you automatically tie your shoes with hardly a thought. Do you remember when you first learned to tie your shoes? Your mother or father may have demonstrated the steps of tying the knot. Did you catch on right away, tie your shoes perfectly the first time? Did you fumble around, going over the steps in your head every attempt, until one day the skill snapped in place in your brain and you just *knew*, from that point on, what to do?

Write down a list of steps for tying your shoes. Work on finishing a well organized, polished set of numbered instructions. Put them in an envelope and set it aside for two weeks. The day you retrieve the envelope, try to *forget* for a few moments how to tie your shoes. Take a pair of shoes with laces, and open the envelope. Read over the rules and follow them step by step. Do you find it difficult or awkward? Which was the more difficult task: tying your shoes automatically or tying your shoes using a list of rules?

Do you believe that we perform most practical tasks such as tying shoes, driving a car or engaging in conversation with people by following rules? Some philosophers, such as Immanuel Kant, understand human behavior to be a rule-governed activity. According to this position, even if you are not conscious of following rules when you *automatically* tie your shoe, you are really following rules that have become habitual so that you do not consciously think about them. Do you think this is true? If there were a difference in how efficiently you tied your shoes when you consciously followed a list of rules than when you did not, would this imply that you only apply rules consciously?

Opposing Kant, Michael Oakeshott (1901-1990), a British philosopher who taught for many years at the London School of Economics, and Hubert Dreyfus (1929-) of the University of California at Berkeley, believe that when a practical skill becomes automatic, you are not following rules. Rules are necessary at the beginning, when you first learn a skill. Your parents were not wasting their efforts when they took you through the steps of tying your shoe. It takes time for you to become skillful enough to tie your shoe without consciously thinking of rules. Dreyfus believes that the process of becoming an expert goes through stages, in which you progressively become less dependent on rules. Once you become an expert at performing a task, you are not following rules at all, even unconsciously. If you, as an expert, attempt to follow rules, you will find that your skill level deteriorates. If you tie your shoes or perform a mundane task such as walking, by rule following, you will tie your shoes less efficiently or your walking will be clumsy.

Are Kant and his followers correct that rules are absolutely essential for doing practical tasks? Or are you more convinced by Oakeshott and Dreyfus, who deny that you are using rules at all once you become an expert? Try doing something else routine, such as walking or engaging in conversation, using a list of rules for these tasks. Do these experiments change your mind?

ADD AND SUBTRACT BY COUNTING MARBLES

Arithmetic is something we take for granted; we *know* that 1 + 1 = 2, 7 + 5 = 12, or 145 — 11 = 134. This knowledge seems absolutely certain, understood by means of reason alone. Arithmetic appears to be known apart from sense experience. You probably do not count beads in your head when you add seven and five.

Philosophers call knowledge which we gain apart from sense experience *a priori* knowledge. Almost all philosophers believe that mathematical knowledge is a priori. It is not only philosophers who hold that our knowledge of reality comes through reason, rather than through sense experience (*rationalists*) who believe this. Even philosophers who think that our knowledge of reality comes through sense experience (*empiricists*) believe that our knowledge of mathematics arises from reason alone. The Scottish philosopher David Hume is often considered to be the most radical of empiricists. For example, he notes that we do not *experience* the future with our senses, but only present events and memories of our sense experiences of past events. Although this seems obvious, Hume went on to claim that this means that we have no basis in sense experience for making predictions about the future, because we cannot know that the future will be like the past. This leads to a skepticism that seems to destroy the reliability of science.

Yet when it comes to mathematics, Hume is not a skeptic at all. He admits that we know that mathematics is true; we know for certain that 7 + 5 = 12 and that the sum of the interior angles of a triangle total 180 degrees. Since Hume is an empiricist, you might think that he would believe that we gain such knowledge by sense experience. But Hume denies this. He believes our knowledge of mathematics comes through reason; it is the way our mind relates ideas into particular patterns, nothing more. Mathematical knowledge is not knowledge of the world that we sense; it is pure thought.

Now try an experiment. Most likely you are used to adding and subtracting small numbers automatically, in your head (if you avoid an electronic calculator, you probably use pen and paper for larger numbers). Think back to the first time you learned to add and subtract. How did you learn? Did you count marbles on the floor inside your home, or count rocks in your back yard? Did you count the pictures of animals sometimes found in beginning arithmetic books? Return to that time. You are learning to count; you may know names of the numbers from one to a hundred. Take twenty marbles and place them on the floor in front of you. Add seven and five, using this method. Take seven marbles, one at a time, counting out loud as you set them aside. Do the same thing with five other marbles. Now, count both groups of marbles continuously until you reach the number twelve.

Moving on to subtraction, count out ten marbles and place them in front of you; then set aside six. Count what is left. Was the result four? Repeat both tasks using the same numbers. If you reach the same answer every time, does this increase your confidence that 7 + 5 will equal 12 in the future, and that 10 — 6 will equal 4 in the future? If so, then have you learned addition and subtraction by sense experience?

The English philosopher John Stuart Mill, like Hume, was an empiricist. Unlike Hume, he believed that we gain mathematical knowledge through sense experience. We would find, for example, that 3 marbles + 2 marbles = 5 marbles, 3 stones + 2 stones = 5 stones - no matter what objects we count, 2 + 3 = 5. Every time the answer comes out the same, our confidence rises that 2 + 3 will equal 5 in the future. We *generalize*, though *induction*, to conclude that 3 + 2 will *probably always* equal 5 in the future. Inductive reasoning is a type of reasoning which only gives us probable conclusions, not certain ones. Thus, if we know mathematics such as arithmetic by induction, we do not know it with absolute certainty, but we do know it with confidence.

Given your experiment with counting marbles, who is right: Hume or Mill? Do you gain knowledge of mathematics by reason or experience? Could there be an alternative view? Does the answer affect your confidence in the reliability of addition and subtraction?

PRETEND A FRIEND IS A ROBOT

Set aside some time this week to have a conversation with a close friend. It is important that you know this person well, including personality, mannerisms, ways of thinking and so forth. There are no restrictions on the subjects you discuss; just engage in an ordinary conversation, as you would on any other day. Try not to be self-conscious as you talk; you do not want your friend or relative to suspect that you are hiding something.

What is it that you know, this dark secret you dare not reveal? Pretend that you know that this *human being* with whom you are talking is a robot. (This exercise is for fun, to stretch your mind, so remember you are only pretending). Perhaps the robot was planted by aliens to better understand human behavior or to scout human vulnerabilities in preparation for an invasion of earth. Maybe it was manufactured by some mad scientist planning to make more robots to replace the human population.

Listen carefully. Do you notice any difference in your friend's voice? What about mannerisms or the ability to express emotions? Is it possible that you notice no difference at all - that someone could be a robot and behave exactly as a flesh and blood human being? The French philosopher René Descartes, a founder of modern philosophy, held that this indeed is possible. He recognized that non-human animals engage in complex behavior. Dogs know how to hunt their prey; chimpanzees engage in complex social behavior. However, Descartes believed that animals are mere machines, robots without thoughts or feelings. Humans think and feel since they have immaterial souls. It is the soul that thinks and feels, not the body, although the soul interacts with the body - and Descartes does not believe that non-human animals have souls. He also denies that you can decide by means of your five senses whether a person with whom you are talking is a human being with a soul. He believes that you can determine this through reason alone.

Is it important whether you are talking to a human being or a robot? A group of philosophers called *functionalists* believe that thoughts and emotions are complex processes which begin with particular inputs (such as a needle prick or words in a conversation). After processing in the brain, the appropriate output results - a feeling of pain and reacting to the pain by withdrawing one's hand or crying out, in the case of the needle prick, or the appropriate response in a conversation. So for the functionalist, it is not important whether an individual has a human or robot body. For all practical purposes, the robot has the same thoughts and feelings as your loved one. If this were true, do you believe that the robot with which you have been talking could be the *same person* as your close friend or relative? If not, would this make any difference?

Suppose a group of benevolent aliens scanned your friend and determined that she was dying. Although they could not cure her body, they transferred her memories into a mechanical body, programming it to behave just as she behaved. The mechanical body is so similar to a human body that you cannot tell the difference - it breathes, has a heartbeat and is warm to the touch. Is this robot your friend? What if the robot cannot think but perfectly imitates your friend's behavior? Would you care that the robot cannot think? Does the fact that the individual with whom you are talking is carrying on a normal conversation lead you to doubt that she really *is* a robot? Does your pretense break down at this point, or do you believe a robot could perfectly imitate human language and conversation without thinking or feeling?

The philosopher and computer pioneer Alan Turing formulated what is now called the *Turing Test*. It is a test designed to determine whether a computer can think. Suppose you are sitting in one room, and in the next room there is either a person or a computer with whom you are carrying on a conversation. Suppose what lies on the other side of the door is a computer. If that computer could carry on a conversation with you so well that you (or any other reasonable person) could not tell that the conversation was really with a computer, according to the Turing Test, the computer can think. Do you agree?

After your conversation with your friend ends, do you have any doubt that you were talking with a human being? Do you ever wonder about you own identity? Do you know for sure that you are not a robot?

DEBATE WITH YOURSELF IN THE MIRROR

Find a full-length mirror and look at your reflection. Say "Hello," and engage yourself in conversation about a controversial topic such as abortion or capital punishment. Ask yourself questions. Answer them; assume that your reflection is your *alter ego* who disagrees with you on every issue. If you favor capital punishment, your reflection disagrees; if you believe in God, your reflection is an atheist. If you are a Democrat, your reflection is a Republican. When you speak the voice of your reflection, present arguments against the position you hold. Avoid arguments that are easy to answer, *straw men*, blown away by a soft wind. Pick the very best arguments against your own position and find the strongest arguments you can to answer them. Then have your alter ego respond to your answers.

When you do this, you are *arguing with yourself*, engaging in a Socratic dialogue with yourself. Socrates, one of the most famous ancient Greek philosophers, developed a method through which he believed people could discover the truth. It is sometimes called the *dialectical method*, a question and answer method. Someone would ask a question, such as "What is beauty?" or "What is justice?" That person would then answer, ideally using arguments to defend what the person believes. Then Socrates would give his answer, usually asking more questions … and so the dialogue goes back and forth. The idea is that by eliminating bad arguments and bad answers, a person can come closer to the truth, although it is difficult in this life to find the whole truth. Socrates practiced this method in Athens, Greece, and dialogued with many people with whom he disagreed. He changed some people's minds, but others stubbornly upheld their positions despite good argumentation against what they believed. Many times they became angry with Socrates.

The dialectical method was designed to be used in conversation between at least two people. So what about your dialogue with yourself while staring into a mirror? Can you have a true dialogue with yourself? Can you really present the best case against your own position? Did you ever become angry with yourself while arguing, as some of Socrates' opponents became angry with him? Do you find that it is necessary for other people to help you hone your arguments for what you believe, or perhaps change your mind about an issue? Do you think you could be convinced by your dialogue with yourself in the mirror to change your position? When you are mulling over a decision in everyday life, do you ever debate with yourself, as if you were two individuals arguing?

There was one significant philosopher who changed the course of philosophy through a dialogue with himself: the *Father of Modern Philosophy*, René Descartes. Alone in a stove heated room, Descartes developed a method though which he believed any person could attain knowledge about philosophy, mathematics, science and medicine. This is the method of doubt - doubting everything possible to doubt. When Descartes found something he could not doubt, he believed he found a sure foundation for knowledge. Descartes doubted the existence of trees, rocks, even his own body, because he might be dreaming. He doubted the truth of mathematics, for an evil demon could be fooling him into thinking that two plus three equals five or that the interior angles of a triangle total 180 degrees when the correct values are something else. But he finally found something he could not doubt: the fact that he is doubting. Since doubting is a form of thinking, he cannot doubt that he's thinking: *I think, therefore, I am* (in Latin, *Cogito, ergo, sum*). This becomes Descartes' foundation from which everything else is proven. From the, *I think*, Descartes attempts to prove both the existence of God and the existence of material things.

Descartes' method of doubt is practiced by a solitary individual. This is a different approach to doing philosophy using Socrates' method, which assumes what the ancient Greeks took for granted, that human beings are naturally social creatures. Which do you believe to be the correct approach? Return to the mirror and debate the issue.

TRY TO THINK WITHOUT IMAGES

When you think, do you have some kind of picture in your mind? For example, if you think *dog*, do you form a mental image of a particular dog? Or do you *see* or *hear* the word *dog* in your mind? Perhaps you experience some other image that is vague. When you add 7 + 5 in your head, do you *see* a *7*, a *5*, and a *12*? Maybe you cannot recall any images at all when you think, or have images of dogs or cats or trees, but not of numbers.

Lie down in a dark, quiet place. Make sure all distracting noises are eliminated: television, radio, stereo and computer should be turned off. If it helps, you can use ear plugs. Wear a blindfold to eliminate as much light as possible. Try to think about these concepts without using any images at all: *cat*, *8 x 7*, and *God*. If you wish to think about other concepts after you finish these three, that is okay. Record your results. Were you able to think without images, even for a brief moment? If so, describe that experience. If not, describe what images your mind perceived. Did you have images for some kinds of concepts but not others? If so, which ones, and how do you explain the difference?

St. Thomas Aquinas did not believe that human beings could think without images being involved in the process of thinking. He thought a pure spirit like God or an angel thinks without sense images. Human beings, however, are embodied; that is, we have physical bodies with sense organs. We are dependent on sense organs in order to gain content about which to think. The mind, by means of the *phantasm*, or sensory image, abstracts the universal content from a given thing. For example, it is by means of the sense image of a dog that I can abstract the universal concept of *dog* and make the judgment, *That creature drinking water from the puddle over there is a dog*. Even when we are not looking at or hearing an object, images in our memory are necessary for the thinking process. Thus, for Aquinas, imageless thinking by human beings is impossible. Given your experience in trying to think without images, do you believe Aquinas is correct?

Oswald Külpe (1862-1915) founded the Würzburg School of Psychology, which accepted the notion of imageless thinking. By studying subjects' reports of the types of thought they had, Külpe concluded that forming images and thinking were two different activities, and that thought can take place without images.

Do you agree with Külpe's position? Is thinking without images possible? Could images be different from thoughts but still be necessary to thought? Can thought dispense of images totally? How do the results of your experience trying to think without images influence your answer?

WATCH THE NEWS

Over a three day period, watch the world news on television on at least three different networks. On a given night, write down the topic from each story. If you are able to record a broadcast on another network at the same time, watch it and write down the topics on that network's news. Most news broadcasts present stories in the order they believe is important. If you are able to compare two broadcasts on the same night, how do their listings of stories compare? If not, check other networks' websites and see what stories they rated as important.

You should also listen for any signs of bias in the stories themselves. Do the news reporters just present *facts*? If you compare broadcasts of the same story, do different networks present the same *facts*? Do reporters have a particular *slant* to a story so that they attempt to get you to think or feel a certain way, or are they completely unbiased?

Walter Cronkite (1916-2009) was for nineteen years anchor of the CBS Evening News. He believed in the ideal of presenting an unbiased broadcast of the news. For the most part, Americans accepted that his broadcasts were accurate and without bias, and he became known as *the most trusted man in America.*

Do you believe it is possible for anyone, even someone who was as trusted as Walter Cronkite, to be completely unbiased in news reporting? What did your experience watching news broadcasts reveal?

The French sociologist Jean Baudrillard (1929-2007) believed there are no facts of the matter when it comes to the world the media presents. He considered that world to be a *virtual reality*, full of conflicting points of view and biases. To Baudrillard, there is no unbiased point of view. Do you agree? How does your analysis of news broadcasts affect your answer? Could there be a mediating position between that of Cronkite and Baudrillard? If so, what is it?

TRY TO WISH AN OBJECT OUT OF EXISTENCE

Would it amaze you to know that some philosophers, including important philosophers, have doubted the existence of a material world? What do you think of that position? Does it seem absurd to you, or is it something about which you have wondered yourself? Maybe there are times you have wondered if you were in a dream or in a world made by computers like the world in the movie *The Matrix*.

Place an object in your field of vision and look at it. Close your eyes and try to wish it away. Get to the point that you know it is no longer there. Then open your eyes. Is the object still there?

The English philosopher John Locke was a *realist*. That is, he believed that the objects we perceive in the world are real material things that would exist even if we are not observing them. He would disagree with any philosopher who doubts the existence of a material world. The test in this exercise was one he suggested as a way to show that material objects really exist. He stated that no matter how much you wish an object away or doubt its existence when you close your eyes, when you open your eyes and look in the same place the object will still be there. Was that the case when you did this exercise?

Locke suggested that if you are unable to wish an object away, it must really exist so it can affect your sense organs and brain. Otherwise, you would not keep seeing an image of the object when you open your eyes. Material objects have a stability that imaginary objects do not. If you imagine a book, and the image of a book appears in your mind, you can easily wish it away. Locke says that is not the case with an actual object. Is this a good test for whether objects really exist outside your mind? Why or why not?

Parmenides, an early Greek philosopher, believed that reality is one (a position called *monism*) and without parts. Reality cannot be known through the senses, but by reason alone. Although there appear to be different objects in the world, that is an illusion. Parmenides would say that any experiment, such as this exercise, based on sense perception will yield illusory results. Only reason can tell us that the world is an absolute unity without any parts. Thus, the experience of your seeing an object on your desk is an illusion, and it does not matter if you are unable to wish it away, since you are still depending on unreliable sense experience.

Is Parmenides correct that the world of our senses is an illusion? Do you think the fact that he would dismiss exercises such as this one shows good reasoning on his part? Would this exercise support Locke or Parmenides, or is it inadequate to answer the question of whether objects we perceive with our senses really exist?

DRAW A BOX

How much of the world you see, hear, touch, taste or smell is really *out there*, and how much does your mind *create* that world? Do things always appear as they really are? Have you been in a situation in which you could not decide what the truth of what you were seeing really was?

Draw a box, like this:

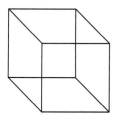

You may have drawn such boxes as a child, or you may still doodle them today if you're in a boring class or a boring meeting at work. Which side of the box is facing you? Does the side facing you change as you gaze at the box? Does the box seem to shift back and forth? Now draw other boxes of the same shape but of different sizes. Do you see the same shifting phenomenon? Look at several boxes at once. What happens?

John Locke believed that the mind received sense data from atoms flowing off material objects and impacting the eye. They reflect, to some extent, what the object is like in reality. Some of the qualities we perceive are literally in the object itself, such as shape and mass - these are the primary qualities. Secondary qualities, such as color and taste, are caused by the way our sense organs and brains act on the primary qualities.

Would shape include which side of a box is facing you? If so, what does this say about Locke's belief that shape is a primary quality? How do you believe Locke would explain the shifting of the sides of the box?

Immanuel Kant believed that the mind brings structure to reality. Without the contribution of our minds, the world would seem to us to be a chaotic mess. But the mind contributes *forms of sensibility*, such as space and time, and *categories of the understanding*, such as causality and substance, to our perception of reality, making our perception orderly and consistent with other people's perceptions. The mind plays a necessary role, not only in our experience of what Locke called *primary qualities*, but in any experience of an object at all. What the object is apart from the ordering of our mind, what the *thing-in-itself* is, is beyond our ability to know. The only world we know is the world ordered by the mind.

What would Kant say about the shifting sides of the boxes? Would his theory of the mind's contribution to reality make better sense of the box phenomena than Locke's theory? How do you make sense of the shifting sides of the box? Does your mind create the shift? If not, what does?

WATCH A SUNRISE

C an you be certain that the sun will rise tomorrow? Of course we take that for granted, but should we? Watch the sun rise one morning. Before it rises, what do you expect to happen? Do you have 100 percent certainty that the sun will indeed rise? If so, what is the basis of your belief? If the sun rises on schedule, does this add to your confidence that the sun will continue to rise in the future?

Aristotle believed in a regular order in nature, an order really out there in the world. Although he would not have understood the sunrise in the same sense we do today, since we hold that the earth revolves around the sun, this would not change his view that the sun will continue to rise in the future. He believed that everything in nature is composed of form and matter. Matter is just a receptacle for form; it is like wax before it receives a seal. The form is similar to the seal in the wax. It gives a thing both the structure it has - for example, your body and its organs are the result of your form - but also the powers an object has to act in certain ways. Because each human being has the form of humanity, everyone lives, eats, has emotions and reasons.

The earth and sun have their forms as well, that give them properties and powers to act in particular ways. Both the sun and earth have gravity that is proportional to their mass. Because of gravity, the earth revolves around the sun. The earth also rotates on its axis, and because this means that about half the earth is illuminated by the sun at any given time, this results in day and night - and in sunrise and sunset. Because the earth and sun have stable properties as the result of their forms, we can be confident that the sun will rise tomorrow.

Do you agree with Aristotle? Do the earth and sun have forms that give them stable properties to the point that we can know that the sun will rise tomorrow?

David Hume disagreed with Aristotle. Hume believed that all we can know through sense experience is that the sun rose in the past - and that it is rising in the present when you actually see it rise. However, sense experience cannot tell you that the sun will rise tomorrow, since we cannot have sense experience of the future. To say that we know that the sun will rise tomorrow assumes that we can know the future from what has happened in the past - but this begs the question, since that is the very point we are considering.

Is Hume correct? If we cannot have sense experience of the future, can we know that the sun will rise tomorrow? Does Aristotle's philosophy have an adequate answer to Hume's? Or is there some other way out of Hume's problem? Relate your answer to your own experience of watching the sun rise.

EXAMINE AN ANCIENT FOSSIL

H ave you ever imagined living in the age of the dinosaurs? Have you thought about taking a time machine 600 million years in the past, diving to the ocean floor and retrieving living trilobites to bring back to the present? Yet the only evidence we have that such creatures were really here are fossils - remains of ancient plants and animals that lived on earth long ago.

Examine a fossil. There are many places to find fossils - you may be able to find some in your own back yard. If not, you can find them in museums and museum shops, as well as in rock and mineral shops. If the fossil you examine is one you can pick up, do so. Imagine what the plant or animal originally looked like. You may check out a fossil book in your local library to identify the fossil; some books have paintings of how the organism may have appeared. Does it seem strange that the rock you are holding in your hand or looking at in a museum was once a living thing millions of years ago? Is it obvious that such a creature actually existed?

John Stuart Mill was a *phenomenalist*; that is, he believed that we do not literally experience external objects with our senses, but rather *sensations*, or *sense data*. What we call a material thing is a bundle of sensations. Yet if that is true, what is the object when we are not looking at it, or not smelling, tasting, hearing or touching it? Mill says that when we are not doing these things, an object continues to exist as *a permanent possibility of sensation*. Take a fossil, for example. When no one is observing the fossil, it continues to exist, not as an actual set of sensations, but as a permanent possibility of sensations. *If* I stand two feet from the fossil and *if* I look at it from a particular angle, *I will see* a particular shape, and *if* I touch the fossil *I will feel* a particular texture.

Yet what about the plant or animal when it actually lived? Many fossils are of creatures that existed before humans appeared on earth. Certainly no human experienced these creatures as living beings. Does that mean they only existed as *permanent possibilities*, that *if* someone had lived during the time the creatures lived and *if* he or she faced the creature, he or she *would experience* certain sensations? But does this position make any sense?

Charles Sanders Peirce, an American philosopher, did not think so.

He argued that if someone found a fossil of an ancient creature the obvious conclusion is that the creature once existed - really existed - as a living creature. Surely, Peirce suggests, the creature was more than a possible collection of sense data - instead, it was a material being with certain real properties and behavior patterns. *Phenomenalism*, Peirce says, must be incorrect and *realism*, in contrast, is the correct view.

After examining a fossil, which view makes better sense to you - Mill's or Peirce's? Why?

CONTEMPLATE, THEN ANALYZE A BELOVED POSSESSION

Why do most people become attached to objects such as heirlooms? Why are many of us sentimental about a beloved toy that we played with as a child or a piece of furniture inherited from a grandparent? Find something you own of which you are particularly fond. Contemplate it. Consider why you love and appreciate it. Then analyze it as a material thing, as an object of science. If it is a toy, try to determine how the toy is put together and analyze the materials out of which it is made. Were the experiences of contemplation and analysis different? Do you believe one should stick only to scientific analysis? After all, a material thing is only good for its usefulness, right? Can there be more to your experience of an object to which you are emotionally attached?

The Jewish philosopher Martin Buber contrasted an *I-It relationship* with an *I-Thou relationship*. Originally he applied this to our view of people - we can treat people as objects and use them, or we can have personal relationships with them and thereby recognize their value. This may be possible with an object you love as well. Either because of a connection to your life, or a connection to someone you love, you may be able to have an *I-Thou relationship* of sorts with a beloved toy or an heirloom that is deeper than mere *scientific* analysis. In a sense, the object is endowed with a kind of dignity it would not ordinarily have. Do you agree with Buber's position? Did you have a sense of an *I-Thou relationship* with the object you chose? Or did the *scientific* analysis make more sense to you?

René Descartes, the great French philosopher who is often considered the founder of modern philosophy, sharply distinguished between the human soul and material objects. The human soul only is where personal dignity and value is located. All material objects are mere matter extended in space and have no personal value. They are subject to scientific analysis. It seems to be the case, if Descartes is consistent, that heirlooms and other material objects could have no transferred dignity; they are mere utilitarian or scientific objects. Is this true? Given the results of your exercise, does Descartes' position make sense to you? Why or why not?

SUSPEND YOUR BELIEF IN AN EXTERNAL WORLD

D o you believe that the world outside your mind really exists? Do you believe that there are material objects *out there* in the world? Most of us probably take these beliefs for granted. After all, when you pick up a bottle of cola, you are picking up an object made of a particular material (usually plastic these days) and drinking a liquid that goes into a material object (your body). Surely all these things are real.

Despite our common sense acceptance of the world of matter, some philosophers have questioned whether we can know there is a world that exists outside of us. This goes beyond questioning the existence of matter - some philosophers believe that everything is made of *mind-stuff* and still think we can know there is a world outside ourselves. But other philosophers are more radical and question whether we can know there is any kind of external world. The Scottish philosopher David Hume is one. Hume believed that we only have experience of sense impressions. But whether there is something behind those sense impressions is a question we cannot answer. For Hume, if I look, for example, at a desk, what I experience is a particular shape, color, texture (if I touch the desk), sound (when I tap the desk) and odor (for example, the odor of fresh varnish). However, we cannot know by our senses that there is any material substance behind those sense impressions. Practically, this does not make a difference - by custom or habit we assume the world is made of stable objects so we do not, for example, run in front of moving automobiles that are too close to us.

Is Hume correct that we cannot know that there is an external world? When you suspended your belief in an external world, did this make any practical difference in your behavior? Does this issue matter?

Aristotle believed that the existence of an external world is something we must take for granted. He considers it mad to even raise the issue since he believes it is obvious that we experience an external world through our senses. Do you agree with Aristotle? Is the point he is making a common sense one or is he engaging in circular reasoning by assuming that an external world exists? Do those who doubt the existence of an external world live consistently with their doubt when they avoid running into objects in their houses? When you doubted the existence of an external world, did you find your practical behavior in tension with your doubt?

Have a Silent Conversation with Yourself

How often have you had a silent internal conversation with yourself? Is that something you find odd? Do you think you need your body to have such a conversation? Does your conversation enrich your own ideas and your life?

Now have a conversation (out loud!) with others on the same topic you talked over with yourself. What was different between the two conversations? Was one more meaningful than the other? Did you feel more personally enriched by one than the other?

For René Descartes, who you are is totally bound up in your individual consciousness. Your body does interact with your mind, but really is not essential to who you are - and neither are other people. You may be able to learn as much from silent conversations with yourself as you would through talking to others. Descartes believed that some of his best work in philosophy was done alone in a stove-heated room. Having a conversation with yourself may not be such a negative thing after all. It might lead to insights you could not gain in any other way.

Is Descartes right? Can a dialogue with yourself enrich your thinking about the world and your life as a whole? Do you need your body or other people to have real conversation? How does your experiment in self-conversation influence your answer?

The Russian literary critic Mikhail Milhailovich Bakhtin (1895-1975) sharply disagreed with Descartes. He believed that having a body is essential to being a human self. It is through the body that we communicate with other people. It is through the body that we develop ourselves through interaction with others. Even a *self-conversation* only makes sense in light of real communication with other people. We learn both our language and habits of action from others, not only from ourselves. Like the ancient Greek Philosopher Aristotle, Bakhtin believes that human beings are naturally social animals. The best way to enrich our knowledge and our lives is not through self-dialogue, but though dialogue with others.

Which thinker makes the most sense to you given your experiment in self conversation: Descartes or Bakhtin?

DESCRIBE EVERYTHING YOU KNOW
ABOUT SOMEONE CLOSE TO YOU

Do you know a person better when you love that person? Does a relationship increase your knowledge of a person? Can you gain knowledge about a person you cannot gain in any other way through loving that person, especially if that person loves you as well?

Describe everything you know about someone close to you. It may be a relative to whom you are particularly close, a close friend or a lover. As you read over your finished description, do you think some of your knowledge of the person arises because of the love relationship that is present?

Thomas Aquinas believed that to know anything, even an inanimate object, there must be some kind of relationship present, some unity between the knower and what he or she knows. For example, to know a particular rock is granite, we first must observe the rock with our senses. The rock has the form *granite*, so by means of the sense image of the rock, our mind *abstracts* the form granite, and in a sense, forms a unity with the rock. We can judge that the rock is *granite*.

For personal relationships, Aquinas thinks a higher form of unity is involved - a unity of love. Through loving a person, we become *conatured* with the beloved and gain a *knowledge through love*, what Aquinas calls *connatural knowledge*, that we cannot gain in any other way. It is not scientific knowledge - it involves much more than describing a person's height and weight and typical behavior. Loving someone is the closest we can get in this life to seeing into the soul of a person. That knowledge is hard to express in language; perhaps poetry or a story could express it better than mere description, but we have to do the best we can.

Do you agree with Aquinas that knowledge through love is the highest form of knowledge of a person? In your experiment, were you able to express knowledge you could not express but for loving the person?

An Australian philosopher, John Anderson (1893-1962) denied that relations contribute to our knowledge in any way. He believed in the *radical independence* of the knower and known. Thus, knowledge cannot, as in Aquinas, refer to the unity of knower and known. There can be no *connatural knowledge*, or *knowledge by love*.

Do you agree with Anderson? Did your experiment fail to reveal knowledge about the person you love that could not be gained in any other way?

PHILOSOPHY OF LANGUAGE

READ A BELOVED BOOK

Pick up one of your favorite books and begin reading. It might be a religious book, such as the Bible or Koran, or a favorite work of fiction, such as *The Lord of the Rings*. If you are a horror fan, you could pick a classic such as *Frankenstein* or a contemporary horror novel such as Stephen King's *Salem's Lot*. If you prefer nonfiction, you might choose a favorite science or history book. It is important that the book is one that you have read before and enjoyed; it is your familiar friend. If it is a novel, you know every plot line; if a history book, you are familiar with every twist and turn.

Do you find new meaning you did not notice before as you reread the book? If so, do you think this happens every time you read it? Is meaning in the book some undiscovered country waiting for you to explore? Is each reading a voyage to a faraway place to which you return time and time again?

Do your expectations of what you will find influence how you interpret the book? Do you think that your background, your family, your religious and political beliefs cause you to read the book differently than someone from a different background? Is it possible that this other person could discover meaning that you missed? Is reading a book something passive, or is it more like a dialogue, a conversation between you and the book in which it "speaks" to you, but you also "speak" to it? How much of the book's meaning is what *you* bring to it, rather than what is *really there*? Is it possible that the *only* meaning in the book is the meaning you bring to it as you read?

A French philosopher, Jacques Derrida, does not believe that there is any *objective meaning* in a text (he calls the idea of an objective meaning a *metanarrative*). Each person creates a unique narrative based on their reading of the text. This reading depends on one's cultural, economic, family and religious background. This means that when you read your book, in a real sense, you *make* its meaning. Derrida's focus is on your *response* to what you are reading. Another person would have a different response, and the meaning of the book would be different for that person.

Do you think Derrida is right? Is meaning only something you give to a text? If so, if you reread a book you have already read, do you give it new meaning each time? Is meaning only your own creation as you read? If so, if you have a conversation with someone else about a book you both love, would you really be able to communicate? If you both give different meanings to the book, could you find any common ground on which to speak?

An alternative position is that meaning is wholly in the book itself. Robert Penn Warren (1905-1989), a major poet and literary critic, believed that meaning is found in the text itself; he accepted the idea of a *metanarrative*. Therefore, the way to discover (not create) such meaning is by a close examination of the text. The reader does not create any meaning in the text that was not there already. Examining the cultural background or biography of the author is worthless for determining the meaning of a text, as is analyzing the reader's background.

Do you agree with Warren? Is meaning in a beloved book created or discovered? Could it be both creation and discovery?

Reread this exercise. Is the meaning in this text something that is there, something I have created? Does it stand on its own apart from you and me, or do you make the meaning of this exercise? If so, does this change how you approach it?

TALK TO SOMEONE IN AN AREA
OUTSIDE YOUR KNOWLEDGE

Have you ever listened to a teacher or an expert in an area with which you are not familiar? Did the person use words you did not understand? Was your experience like exploring an unfamiliar place? Why do you think it is sometimes difficult to understand experts in different areas?

Talk to someone who is an expert in a field you do not know or do not know well. If you are a concrete thinker, talk to a philosopher. If you love science but know little about literature, talk with an English professor. If you are mechanically challenged, talk to an automobile mechanic. If you do not know the difference between the pancreas and the pituitary, talk to a medical doctor. Ask the expert questions about his or her field. If the expert uses unfamiliar terms, ask for an explanation.

Was your experience a difficult one, in which you were unable to understand the expert? Or did you learn a great deal about the expert's field? Did you learn the meanings of words you did not know before? Did you learn about familiar words used in unfamiliar ways? Did it seem as if you and the expert were speaking different languages? Did you feel as if you and the expert were living in completely different worlds?

A. J. Ayer (1910-1989) believed that language could only be used in two ways.

First, it could be used to refer to tautologies, statements that are always true such as, *A cat is a cat* or *7 + 5 = 12*. Second, it could refer to states of affairs (a fancy term for things or events in the world) that are empirically verifiable by our five senses. Language should have a precise meaning, whether it is mathematical, scientific or practical. Ultimately we all live in one linguistic world. Did you find this to be true when you interviewed an expert? Was the expert's linguistic world the same as yours?

In the later work of Ludwig Wittgenstein we find a different view of language. People live in different linguistic worlds which determine, to a large extent, how they use language. This does not mean that people in different fields are unable to communicate, since there are *family resemblances* between different uses of language (what Wittgenstein labels *language games*). But it does mean that an English professor may have trouble communicating to someone who works in physics, and vice versa. Each field of study or practice has its own vocabulary, its own way to foster communication between experts in the same field. Medical doctors have a specialized vocabulary, but so do automobile mechanics and literature professors. In a sense, people in these communities live in different *linguistic worlds*. Even if people in different areas of expertise use the same words, they may define them in different ways.

Is Wittgenstein correct? Did doing this exercise give you any insight on whether Ayer or the later Wittgenstein is correct?

CONSTRUCT AN IDEAL LANGUAGE

H ave you noticed that words sometimes have different meanings? Has someone misunderstood you because you used a word in one way and the other person understood it in a different way? Wouldn't it be a good thing if we could communicate without ambiguity? Fewer misunderstandings would mean fewer lost friendships and, more importantly, fewer conflicts between nations. Is it possible to modify language so that it is completely clear in meaning?

We all know words that have multiple meanings. The word *bank* can mean a bank into which you put money, the bank of a river or it can be used as a verb. The word *love* can mean romantic love, friendship love, parental love and it has many other meanings. If you have ever meant, *I love you*, in one way and the person who heard you took it another way, you realize how language can get you (and other people) in trouble.

Try to develop an ideal language. Come up with a list of new words: ten nouns, ten verbs and ten adjectives. Define them, and stipulate that the definition you give is the *only* way to define those words. Keep the same articles we already use in English - *a*, *an* and *the*. Keep also the same pronouns. Now write a short paragraph in your ideal language. Then write another paragraph about a different subject matter. For example, if your first paragraph was about sports, write you second paragraph about religion, art or physics (to give some examples). Compare the two paragraphs. Do the meanings of your nouns shift or do they remain the same. Does your new language avoid all ambiguity?

The German philosopher Gottfried Leibniz believed that he could develop *a characteristica universalis*, a universal and ideal language that avoids all ambiguity. He thought that such a contribution would contribute to world peace and harmony between people and nations by removing sources of misunderstanding due to the ambiguity of word meanings and the ambiguity of language in general. Did your experiment show that he could be right?

The later work of the Austrian-born British philosopher Ludwig Wittgenstein questioned the possibility of developing an ideal language. Wittgenstein believed that we play different *language games* depending on the use which we made of language. The language game of physics will not be the same as the *language games* of art or religion. Words may not mean the same thing across different games, and this is perfectly acceptable. This implies that it is impossible to develop an ideal language in which words do not shift meaning, since such variation is unavoidable across language games.

Do you agree with Wittgenstein? Did your using *different language games* in this exercise reveal shifts in word meaning? If so, does this imply Leibniz is correct? If not, does this support Wittgenstein's position?

COMPARE GOOD THINGS

Find some things you consider to be *good*. There is no limit on the kind of object you find - it could be a good book, a good television, a good board game, a good dog or cat, good food, a good desk. Place as many of these good things side by side as you can. Now, think of those people you consider to be *good people*. Write down the characteristics of all these things, animals and people that make them *good*. Compare the characteristics. Are there any commonalities? If so, what are they? How do the lists differ? Can you sort out the commonalities and differences and write a definition of the word, *good*? If so, what is your definition? If not, why not? Have a friend do the same thing. Compare your results. Ask your friend questions about the nature of goodness based on your friend's experience with this experiment. Make sure both you and your friend justify your answers.

Plato believed that there is an *essence* to Goodness - you can find the one correct definition for Goodness. By examining good things and good people and engaging in a dialectical, question and answer method with another person, you can discover what Goodness really is. Then, you will realize that Goodness Itself does not exist on earth; instead, it exists as the *Form of Goodness* in a world that transcends our own. Objects on this earth only *participate* in the Form of Goodness. Do you agree with Plato? Consider the results of your experiment in your answer.

Ludwig Wittgenstein, an Austrian philosopher who later taught at Cambridge University in England, had a different approach to words like *good*. There cannot be one unique definition of *good* or *goodness*. How we define *good* depends on the object we are labeling "good." So the meaning of *good* in *good game* differs from the meaning in *good iced tea*, which in turn differs from the meaning of *good person*. There is no common essence to be found in goodness. However, this does not imply that there is no commonality between the various uses of the word "good." There may be certain *family resemblances* between the uses of "good,", and we can learn something about how we use the word "good" if we consider those similarities and differences.

Given your experience in the experiment with good things, who makes more sense to you, Plato or Wittgenstein? Why? Does your friend agree with you? If so, why? If not, what reasons does your friend give?

READ FROM A TECHNICAL MANUAL
THEN READ POETRY

We take language for granted. We communicate with others through speech and writing, and most of the time we do not think twice about it. We do our thinking in language. Yet the origins of language remain shrouded in mystery. Was there an original language that developed into all the languages we have today? What about the many ways we use language today? There are technical languages, there is religious language, poetic language, scientific language, emotional language, the practical language of everyday life. Could all these uses of language have originally started with one use? In addition, if we think through language, was there originally only one form of thought?

Read from a technical manual. A good manual to use would be one of the manuals for your computer or for computer software. Now find a book of poetry and read a few pages from it. What were the differences between technical language and the language of poetry? What are the differences between the kinds of thinking found in both languages? Could technical language and the thought behind it have originated in poetic language, or vice versa? Or are they completely separate uses of language?

Martin Heidegger, a German philosopher, was among the most important twentieth century philosophers. In his later writings, he claimed that all other forms of language were parasitic (or drew their *nourishment* from) poetry. Unlike technology, which reduces everything to something that can be used, poetic language reveals reality to us and shows us the holy. All thought was once poetic, all language was once poetic, and there is a need to recover this original use of language today.

Is Heidegger correct? Does poetry reveal things in their full truth? Do technology and its language hide reality in a language focusing on using things? Does technical language draw all its energy from poetry? Do all other uses of language do the same?

Another great twentieth century philosopher, Ludwig Wittgenstein, believed that language has a number of uses and that this is a good thing. Sometimes we use poetic language, at other times religious language, at other times technical language. Which *language game* we play depends on what we are doing with language. Language is a tool that is flexible and which must be modified and stretched to perform certain tasks. There was no original "pure language," whether of poetry or science.

Is Wittgenstein correct about language? What was your experience reading the technical manual and then reading poetry? Did you find both uses of language to be useful depending on the context? Or did you find one better? Is there an original ideal language, whether poetic or scientific?

ETHICS

WHAT DIFFERENCE WOULD IT MAKE
IF YOU HAD NEVER EXISTED?

W hat if you had never existed? What kind of difference, if any, would it make? In the movie, *It's a Wonderful Life*, George Bailey is about to commit suicide - but then an angel, Clarence, takes him on a journey through the past and shows him how the world would be different if he had never lived. His wife, Mary, would have lived her life as a lonely, bitter woman. Without George's generosity, the town, Bedford Falls, would have fallen under the control of the greedy, evil Mr. Potter. And if George had not existed, he would not have been there to save his brother from drowning - his brother, who would later become a war hero.

Most of our lives do not involve saving someone from drowning or protecting a town from evil. Most of us will not become world leaders. You are one of over five billion people on earth today, and there have been billions more who died in the past. So what difference would it make if you - or I - had never been born?

If you have children, the first thought that might go through your mind is, *My children would not exist if I had never existed.* That is true - *your* children would not exist, though the person with whom you had children could have had children with someone else. What if you plan to have no children? What if you do not plan to do anything grand, but only wish to live a simple life with a regular nine-to-five job. You are a reasonably good person who treats others with decency and respect, but suppose that you have no aspirations beyond the average, and that is okay with you. What if no one remembers you fifty years after your death? Think about this: do you know the names of any of your ancestors before your grandparents? You might try researching your family history; you may find, as I did, that most of my ancestors are long forgotten, many buried in unmarked or neglected graves. You would not exist without an ancestor, but if your fate is to be as forgotten as they are, is your existence really that important?

The English poet and essayist John Donne (1572-1631) said, *No man is an island, entire of itself.* He believed that human lives are interconnected, so that when a person dies, it diminishes all of us. The idea is that one thing that makes our lives significant is our *relationships* with other people - parents, spouses, other family members, friends, even strangers. Without you, the relationships dependent on your existence would never have come to be. Do you think that your friends' lives would be the same without you, without the relationship which enriches both of you? This emphasis on relationship is common to major religions, such as Buddhism, Christianity and Hinduism. If your life affects those around you in a positive way, these effects can reverberate to more people, as *It's a Wonderful Life* suggests. Thus, your life makes a difference to the world, and it would matter if you had never existed. Do you agree with Donne?

Does it matter to you that other people exist? What if no human beings ever existed? What if the universe is pointless? The English philosopher Bertrand Russell said that all human achievements shall be destroyed in the final death of the universe. But he still believed that it is worthwhile to exist. Why? If human life really does not matter, what would this imply for your own existence?

Maybe your view of reality, your *world view*, can help you to answer the question of whether it would matter had you not been born. Maybe you believe that you are created in the image of God, and that you have a purpose planned by this God. If this is true, then your existence matters and that it would make an almost infinite difference if you had not been born. Your life should be spent in service to God and your fellow human beings. Perhaps you believe that there is no God, but each one of us must do our small part to make the world a better place. Or you might believe that life is meaningless and that it really would not matter if you had been born, but since you are here, you might as well make your own meaning in life, a view similar to atheistic existentialist philosophers such as Jean Paul Sartre and Albert Camus. On the other hand, perhaps you think that, since it does not matter if you exist, you might as well seek all the pleasure you can. Imagine again you never exist, now taking your world view into account. Does it make any difference?

Imagine You Do Not Know
into Which Family You Will be Born

This is an exercise in imagination. Try to follow the directions as closely as possible. Imagine you are standing in an empty, white room. Although you are naked you are neither male nor female. Other people in that room look exactly the same as you. Suddenly a voice rings out. The voice says, "You are in place of waiting. Soon you will be born somewhere on the planet Earth. You do not know whether you will be a man or woman. You do not know what color your skin will be. You do not know whether you will have enough to eat, or whether you will be rich or poor. Before you are allowed to be born, you must decide as a group what system of justice you want to establish for the time you will live on earth. When you decide, I will release you to be born into the family I have chosen for you."

What would you do? Perhaps some individuals in the group would set up an orderly system of conversation, and you could mutually decide the rules of a just society. What rules would you support?

John Rawls (1921-2002), a Harvard philosopher, imagined a world similar to the one just described, one he labeled *the original position*. He did not believe that such a world really existed; this was a thought experiment to determine the fairest system of justice in the real world. Rawls primarily had in mind *distributive justice*, the fairest way to distribute resources such as food, clothing, shelter and other goods among the people. Rawls thought that people in the original position would set up a world with *the principle of equal liberty*. This principle says that everyone has equal liberty that is compatible with the same kinds of liberties for others in society. Rawls also accepted *the difference principle*. That says that distribution of resources would be to the benefit of the least advantaged people, such as the poor. He thought that people in the original position would accept the difference principle because any one of them might be born poor and be in need of aid. Do you agree with Rawls? Is this the system of justice you would set up in your world?

Michael Sandel (1953-), another Harvard professor, believes there is a deep flaw in Rawls' original position. He suggests that there is no way we can pretend that we are people without any attachments to other people, especially to our families. Human beings, he believes, are social in nature and cannot isolate themselves, even in a thought experiment, from the relationships into which they are born. If Sandel is correct, Rawls' original position cannot even get off the ground.

With whom do you agree: Rawls or Sandel? When you imagined the original position, did you slip in information about yourself, such as your sex or family situation, that was forbidden by the rules of the game? If so, try the exercise again. Assuming you are able to imagine yourself without any attachments, what happens when you engage in conversation with other people? Are you able to imagine them as sexless, without any attachments? What does this exercise say about your views on human nature? Can we make sense of a human being without attachments of any kind or are we naturally social animals?

THINK OF THE HAPPIEST DAY OF YOUR LIFE

W hat was the happiest day of your life? Search your memory. If you discover more than one equally happy day, choose one of these. Was it a day as a child in which you jumped into mud puddles after a hard rain? Was it the day you first fell in love? Perhaps it was the day your play helped win a big game for an athletic team or the day you were accepted into college. It may have been a day in which you found religious faith or a day in which you lost religious faith.

Ask some friends to describe the happiest day of their lives. How closely do their experiences of happiness match yours? What do the answers suggest concerning you and your friends' conceptions of happiness? Does a person's position on what is really important in life make any difference on how he or she perceives *happiness*?

Jeremy Bentham (1748-1832) believed that there was one correct definition of happiness - *happiness* is the same thing as *pleasure* and *unhappiness* is the same thing as *pain*. Looking back to the happiest day of your life, do you believe that your happiness was wholly a matter of feeling pleasure? Ask your friends the same question. Do they believe that happiness is the same thing as pleasure?

Now consider the question of whether happiness *equals* pleasure or whether pleasure is a *byproduct* of happiness. Does this possibility encourage you to consider changing your views on the relationship between happiness and pleasure?

Aristotle did not identify happiness with pleasure. He did not deny that pleasurable sensations may follow from happiness, but for him, happiness was much more than a series of pleasurable feelings. He used a Greek word, *eudaimonia*, for happiness. *Eudaimonia*, for Aristotle, refers to a life well-lived, a life of a person with good character. If you are a good person, but suffer some painful experiences, you could still be happy in Aristotle's sense. On the other hand, if you are a bad person, you are unhappy, even on a day you later consider to be the happiest day of your life.

Is Aristotle correct in his view that happiness depends on character? Can you be in pain and still be truly happy, or have pleasurable feelings and really be unhappy? Do you believe that most people today would agree with Bentham or with Aristotle? Does the answer you gave to the question of the happiest day of your life support Bentham's or Aristotle's position? What about your friends' answers?

BE APATHETIC

The title of this exercise may seem strange. Can you imagine your parents telling you, "We'd like you to be more apathetic today?" Would your teachers or your boss ever say, "You're not apathetic enough." To be *a* (without) *patheia* (passion) seems to imply not caring about anything, not having any motivation to accomplish one's tasks.

Now, try to be apathetic in the sense of not caring. That is, for one day, do not allow negative events in life to disturb your peace of mind (if a serious crisis event occurs, such as a severe illness or a death in the family, you should not do this exercise). If someone is rude to you or you get a flat tire, do not allow these events to disturb you. Do not react to them emotionally. Want whatever happens to you to happen. If you forget to take your umbrella to the store and get wet, tell yourself, "That's what I really wanted to happen."

If something good happens to you, continue to be apathetic. Too much excitement might interfere with your peace of mind. So if something good happens, tell yourself, "This is what I wanted to happen. But rather than having an emotional outburst of joy, I'll be calm and take it easy."

Epictetus (55?-135?), a Stoic philosopher, believed that the most important quality for a person to develop is what he called *ataraxia*, or what we might call *peace of mind*, which has a meaning close to that of *apatheia*, which literally means *without emotion*. He believed that we cannot control external events that happen to us. For example, if a store clerk is rude to you for no good reason, you could not have controlled that clerk's reaction. If your car has a flat tire, you cannot control that event. But you can react to those events in an appropriate way by realizing that since you do not have power over these events, you might as well relax and take them as they come. There is no sense in desiring what you cannot control. Once the tire on your car is flat, you can change the flat and move on, but you cannot change the fact that the tire became flat in the first place. Why waste time wishing your tire had not gone flat? The same applies to the good things that happen to us. We cannot control them, either, so we should not have emotional outbursts as if we could. Do you agree with Epictetus' perspective? How does your experiment in *passionlessness* affect your answer?

Thomas Aquinas sharply disagrees with Epictetus and the Stoics' notion of apathy. He agrees with the Stoics that we can have an excess of desire for things and that excess desire is wrong. However, he also believes we can have too little desire, a state he calls *apathy*. Aquinas, unlike Epictetus, who believed only in a universal natural law that is neither good nor evil, believed in a personal creator God who is good. Since God is good, everything that He created is good. We should desire God first and other good things in life second, and have a proper level of passion for these things. For Aquinas, apathy is a serious sin, since it leads a person to be apathetic about God, whom Aquinas believes to be a person's highest good. Lacking passion for the good things that happen in our lives is wrong as well, for it is a sign of ingratitude to our Creator. Although we should not be excessive in our passions, we should not desire peace of mind at the expense of passions that are both healthy and good.

Given your experience of *ataraxia*, do you agree more with Epictetus or with Aquinas?

Rate Activities on a Pleasure-Pain Scale

C an pleasures and pains be rated on a numerical scale? Try it. Do something you enjoy. It could be as simple as eating a chocolate chip ice cream cone, if you like that flavor. Now write out the seven attributes listed below and rate the pleasure on a 1-10 scale on each attribute.

- **Intensity:** how intense was the pleasure?
- **Duration:** how long did the pleasure last?
- **Certainty:** how certain were you that the activity in which you engaged would result in pleasure?
- **Propinquity:** how soon after you engaged in the activity did the feeling of pleasure occur - the sooner the pleasure occurred, the higher rating you give this attribute.
- **Fecundity:** does your activity lead to only one pleasure or to many other pleasures? The greater the number of resulting pleasures, the higher you rate this attribute.
- **Purity:** does your activity result only in pleasure, or is the pleasure mixed with pain? The less the pleasure is mixed with pain, the higher you rate this attribute.
- **Extent:** does your activity lead others to feel pleasure, or is it something that only gives pleasure to yourself? The more people who receive pleasure from your activity, the higher you rate this attribute.

Now total the numbers; you will have a rating between 1 and 70. Now do some other activities you enjoy and rate them. Have a group of friends do the same activities and see if their numerical ratings for each activity are close to yours.

Now do something you dislike - perhaps eating Brussels sprouts or cleaning your room. Rate it on the same scale, but with the amount of pain being the unit of measure rather than the amount of pleasure. Try other activities you dislike and rate them, too. Have your friends try the same activities and rate them. Compare the ratings. It might be the case that your friends rate some activities as pleasurable that you find painful and vice versa. Did that ever happen?

You have just used the *hedonic calculus* developed by the British philosopher Jeremy Bentham. Bentham was attempting to establish ethics as a science - a science with the same mathematical precision as physics. He believed that an action is right if and only if it leads to the greatest pleasure and least amount of pain for the greatest number of people, the *principle of utility*. He held you could rate pleasures or pains quantitatively, using an exact mathematical scale. Given your experiment, do you believe that it is possible to accurately measure pleasures and pains this way?

John Stuart Mill was a follower of Bentham who modified some of Bentham's positions. He agreed with Bentham that a person needs to calculate the amount of pleasure and pain resulting from a particular action. But unlike Bentham, he did not believe that one could place an exact numerical value on the amount of pleasure or pain resulting from a given activity. However, a person could make a roughly accurate estimation of the pleasure or pain resulting from actions by observing not only one's own reactions, but those of his or her immediate circle of acquaintances.

Is Mill correct that although an exact numerical estimation of pleasure or pain is not possible, a reasonably accurate estimation remains possible? Look back at the results of your experiment. Do you think the results support Bentham, Mill or neither philosopher?

WHAT DO YOU DESIRE ABOVE ALL THINGS?

W hat is it you desire more than anything in the world? Is it a stable family, wealth, fame, visiting another country, friendship, romance, a relationship with God or something else? Gather a group of friends and each one of you write down what you desire more than anything else in the world. Compare the answers.

Now ask yourself, "What if I do not reach my desire?" Would you feel bad? If you have not attained what you desire, are you impatient to do so? If you have attained what you desired, what was it like? Was it satisfying or disappointing? Do desire and pain ever go together?

These may seem like strange questions, for many people believe that desire is a good thing. It drives us to reach our goals. Some desires, such as the desire for food and drink, are required for our lives, as well as human life in general, to go on. Sexual desire is essential for the human species to continue. Other desires, such as the desire to work toward the goal of employment, are important to most of us for a successful life.

Yet not all thinkers have believed desire to be a good thing. Siddhartha Gautama (c. 560-480 B.C.) was an Indian prince who lived a sheltered life in his youth. After marriage and having a son, he decided, at age 29, to go outside the palace, where he saw an old man, a sick man, a rotting corpse and an ascetic. The experience shocked him into becoming an ascetic himself. Eventually, while sitting under a Bodhi tree, he attained enlightenment and from that point on was called *The Buddha*, which means *The Enlightened One*.

The Buddha believed that all existence is suffering and that suffering comes from our desires. If we work on getting rid of our desires through the *eightfold path*, eight rules involving both living a good moral life and meditative practices, we can attain *Nirvana*, or complete absence of desire. We can do this because nothing is permanent in the world - everything is constantly changing. We do not even have permanent selves. If what we desire is ultimately unreal, then we should understand that desire is pointless and only causes pain from frustration at not attaining what we want or expect.

Is the Buddha right? Is desire pointless? Do the things we desire change so much that attaining them is pointless? Imagine yourself not desiring anything. What would that be like?

Aurelius Augustinus, or St. Augustine, was a Christian and Bishop of Hippo in North Africa. He disagrees with the Buddha that all desires are wrong. Desires are good if they are in the correct order. For Augustine, that means desiring God above all finite things. Augustine would go along with the Buddha as far as admitting that everything finite and limited is not permanent, and if we desire such limited things above God, they will be unsatisfying and cause pain. In addition, Augustine believes that our desires became disordered when Adam and Eve sinned in the Garden of Eden, spreading the infection of sin to the entire human race. Desire, or concupiscence, becomes twisted, and we want wealth or sex or fame above God. When God saves us, our desires can be put in their proper place, with desire for God on top and desire for finite things considered less important.

Is Augustine correct to believe that desiring God is more important than other desires? Do you believe this downplays finite desires too much? Between the two thinkers, the Buddha or Augustine, with whom are you more sympathetic? How did your exercise with your friends influence your answer?

LIVE SIMPLY FOR ONE WEEK

Have you wondered what life would be like if you didn't have to worry about feeling pain or pleasure? Can the life of seeking pleasure and avoiding pain just be tiring sometimes? For one week (or for a day or two if you would prefer), live a simple life that fulfills only the most basic needs. Do not listen to music, do not surf the Internet, do not text on your phone, do not watch television. Eat only bland food such as plain bread or unseasoned rice. Drink water or milk, but avoid coffee and carbonated beverages. Avoid as many physical pleasures as possible. Sleep in a spot that is uncomfortable, but not painful.

What was the experience like? Was it rewarding, painful or neutral? Do you consider this kind of simplified life to be the good life? Why?

Diogenes of Sinope (c. 400-325 B.C.) was an ancient Greek philosopher who founded a school of philosophy known as *The Cynics*, from the Greek word for dog, *kune*. Diogenes had contempt for both pleasure and pain, and lived the simplest kind of existence. Allegedly he lived in a bathtub. Contempt for one's pleasure and pain is a sign of self control, that one is not a slave to either pleasure or pain.

Do you agree with Diogenes? Did you have a sense of mastering your desires when you lived simply? Or is Diogenes' view wrong-headed? If so, why?

Epicurus was the founder of (surprise!) *Epicureanism*. He believed that the only thing good in itself is pleasure and the only thing bad in itself is pain. Thus, we should seek pleasure and avoid pain. This does not mean that we should relish sensual pleasures to excess, such as too much alcohol or sex, since excess can lead to less pleasure in the end. However, it does mean that we should seek moderate pleasures, especially friendship, good conversation and moderation in food and drink. Epicurus would consider Diogenes' contempt for pleasure or pain as contrary to human nature, since human beings naturally seek pleasure and avoid pain.

Is Epicurus correct in his view that we should seek pleasure and avoid pain? How would Diogenes answer Epicurus' views? Given your experience living like a Cynic, do you believe Diogenes or Epicurus to be closer to the truth?

TRY TO LOVE SOMEONE YOU HATE

Have you ever hated anyone? Most of us probably have, even if we do not think it is right to hate another human being. Do you believe it is possible to love and hate someone at the same time? Does your answer depend on how you define *love* and *hate*? If so, how do you define these words?

If you do hate anyone, try to love that person. Are you able to do so? What if you do nice things for that person even when the person treats you badly? Suppose you are feeling rage and intense dislike for the person while you are doing those nice things. Does that mean you have succeeded in loving that person?

Immanuel Kant distinguishes two types of love: *pathological love* and *practical love*. *Pathological love* does not refer to some kind of disease but to emotional love. You feel *pathological love* when you are romantically in love or when you feel deep affection for a family member or close friend. *Pathological hatred* would be when you feel intense dislike for a person. However, *practical love*, what Kant takes to be love in the true and highest sense, occurs when you treat someone as *an end in him/herself* rather than a means to an end. If you treat a person with respect and dignity, even if you feel pathological hatred for that person, you still have practical love for that person. In a way, you can love someone (practical love) and hate someone (pathological hate) at the same time. You could also feel pathological love for someone and not have practical love, such as being romantically in love but using the lover to feel better about oneself, rather than treating the lover with due respect.

Now that you know these distinctions, do you think you were able, in your experiment, to love someone you hate? Do you agree with Kant's view of love?

The Greek philosopher Aristotle agrees with Kant to the extent that he thinks love involves more than mere feelings. It also involves duties to the family members and friends we love and treating them with respect. However, Aristotle believes that we are not obligated to love evil people, those who lack virtue or good character. Although criminals may have a twisted form of love, the highest form of love, expressed in friendship, can only take place between good people. Aristotle is more restricted than Kant on whom we can love. If you hate someone who is evil because he or she is evil, then you cannot really love that person, even practically.

Is Kant or Aristotle more truthful on the nature of love? How does your experiment in trying to love someone you hate play into your answer?

Intentionally Choose
the Worst of Two Choices

Can a person intentionally chose what he or she believes is bad? Does a smoker, for instance, choose to smoke cigarettes knowing they are bad, or does the person smoke them because the smoker believes they are good? What about people who make bad moral choices. Does the bank robber think he is doing evil when he robs the bank?

Make a choice you consider to be bad - not a bad moral choice, but something more trivial. Suppose you love chocolate ice cream but hate vanilla ice cream. Then choose to eat vanilla ice cream. Or you could walk out into a rain without an umbrella, or into snowy weather without wearing a hat. Did you think the choice you made was bad when you made it? Or did you think it good, since you are doing it to fulfill this exercise?

Plato, the Greek philosopher who set the stage for almost all future philosophy, believed that no one could willingly choose to do a bad thing. Both evil moral actions and nonmoral actions that cause harm to us if we perform them are done due to ignorance. If someone robs a bank, it is because that person is ignorant that it is wrong to do such a thing. If someone's health goes downhill due to poor diet and lack of exercise, it is because of ignorance that a good diet and regular exercise helps a person stay healthy.

Do you agree with Plato that no one willingly does what is wrong? What about the choice that you made? Did you know it was a bad choice when you made it? Are there other examples from your experience that would support or oppose Plato's theory?

Aristotle, Plato's student, disagreed with his master. Aristotle thought that people can willingly choose to do bad things, even though they know they are bad. However, he also believed that they always see some good arising from the bad thing, even though they might intellectually know the choice they make is ultimately bad. For example, a smoker may enjoy the pleasure of nicotine, even knowing that she may get cancer, emphysema or heart disease from smoking cigarettes. The adulterer may choose a few moments of intense pleasure, even though he may know if he is discovered, it will cause heartache for a number of people. What about your experience when you choose the wrong thing? Did you know it was bad but still choose it for the good that came out of it? Is it possible to make a choice knowing it is bad and not expecting any good out of that choice? Do you agree more with Plato or Aristotle?

DEBATE A MORAL ISSUE WITH A FRIEND

I s morality merely a matter of one's feelings, or does morality gives us knowledge, even if such knowledge is not *scientific* knowledge? Find a friend with whom you know you disagree sharply about a moral issue. Perhaps the issue is abortion, euthanasia or whether it is right to cheat on a test. Each of you debate the issue for an hour. Then go back and list the reasons each of you had for supporting a particular position. Was the debate more than name calling? Were reasons given for each position? If so, is this significant?

The British philosopher A. J. Ayer believed in a theory of ethics called *emotivism*. That is, morality is nothing more than a set of expressions about emotion. Ayer believed this because of his position that the only meaningful statements were either those that we could verify by sense experience or tautologies (necessary truths, such as *A dog is a dog* or, for Ayer, mathematical expressions such as *7 + 5 = 12*). A moral statement cannot be tested by our five senses to determine whether it is true. For example, we can say, *John Doe shot Charlie Doe after stealing his money*, and that statement can be empirically verified. But saying *John Doe ought not to have murdered Charlie Doe* cannot be verified by the senses, nor is it a tautology. Thus, for Ayer, it is a meaningless expression of emotion. *Murder is wrong* simply means, *Murder - I don't like it!*

Is Ayer right? When you debated with your friend, was your debate just a battle over emotions with no cognitive content? Why or why not?

A different view of morality was presented by the British writer C. S. Lewis (1898-1963). Lewis stated that when people argue about morality, they give rational reasons why they hold the position they do. For example, if you are opposed to cheating on a test, you might say that it is unfair to other students who have studied to have a student who failed to study make an A by cheating. That statement is more than an expression of emotion. Arguments about morality, Lewis suggests, would be literally nonsense if they were only expressions of emotion instead of making use of reasonable arguments. Thus, Lewis concludes, morality is cognitive, telling us something about how we ought to behave in the world. There are *moral facts*.

Is Lewis correct? Does your debate over a moral issue lead you to support Lewis's position or Ayer's? Why?

YOU AND YOUR FRIENDS DEVELOP
A SYSTEM OF MORALITY

Is morality absolute? Are there objective moral standards that apply to all cultures, or is morality relative to the culture? Maybe morality is relative to the individual and not only to the culture. But if that is the case, how can we get along in a world that seems full of moral rules?

Get together with a group of friends and develop a moral system. Set up some rules that you believe people should follow. Have your friends do the same. Then have a debate among yourselves to develop a list of moral rules on which all of you agree.

What was the result of your exercise? Was it easy to come to an agreement? Were you able to come up with any list at all, or did you end up stuck in disagreement? If you came up with a list of rules on which you agreed, do you and your friends believe every human being should follow those rules, or only a subset of humans? If so, which subset?

Ruth Benedict (1887-1948) was an anthropologist who believed that morality is relative to a particular culture. She appealed to the differences in moral standards across cultures to argue that there are no moral standards that apply to everyone. Because cultures develop in different ways due to their unique histories, they have unique moral codes. It is wrong to apply the moral rules of one culture to another culture.

Is Benedict correct in her cultural ethical relativism? In your exercise, do you believe the rules you and your friends came up with only apply to that group? Or do they apply to other groups and to other people?

The German philosopher Immanuel Kant developed a form of ethics called *deontological ethics*. He believed that moral rules apply because they are right and not because of any consequences that arise from following or not following those rules. He also believes that moral rules apply to all rational beings - and that includes all human beings. From reason arises the *categorical imperative*, which says that we should act on rules that we can universalize, that is, apply to everyone, without contradicting ourselves. For example, everyone should keep their promises, since a moral rule against promise keeping would imply that a *promise is not a promise*. This makes no more sense than saying *a cat is not a cat*. So a moral rule about promise keeping must apply to all people, no matter what culture they're in. Other moral rules also apply to all people in all times and all places.

Do you agree more with Benedict or Kant? Were you and your friends able to use your reason to come up with clear moral principles? How does the result of your experiment influence whether you accept the position of Benedict or of Kant?

Aesthetics

COMPARE RESPONSES TO A PAINTING

Find a painting you believe to be beautiful. It may be in a book of paintings, or it may be hanging on your wall. Ask yourself, *Why is this painting beautiful?* Give your reasons. Is the painting beautiful because it makes you feel good in some way? Is there some feature about the painting itself that makes it beautiful? Perhaps you like the colors, or perhaps there is a symmetry and order in the painting you find attractive.

Now show the painting to a friend and ask your friend whether the painting is beautiful. Suppose your friend agrees with you. In that case, ask your friend to list the reasons why. Does your friend's reasoning agree with yours?

Suppose your friend believes that the painting is ugly or *okay* or *just average*. Ask your friend to explain why. If your friend believes that the painting is ugly, are you offended by this? Do you believe that other people should agree with your judgment about the beauty or ugliness of a painting?

Immanuel Kant believed judgments of beauty are subjective. He thought that a beautiful object causes a person to feel pleasure. Yet Kant also believed that judgments of beauty are universal. That is, when you feel an object is beautiful, you expect everyone else to agree with you. Is Kant correct? Is the belief that a painting is beautiful, ugly or *just average* based on a feeling? Did you expect your friend to agree with you about the painting?

Although he was not a fan of works of art, Plato did believe that judgments of beauty are objective. He thought that if you call an object *beautiful*, you are appealing to some ultimate standard of *Beauty*. Philosophers like Plato have looked to proportion, order and symmetry among the parts of a beautiful object as standards by which we can judge an object to be beautiful. Do you agree? Are there features in a painting itself that make it beautiful? If you and your friend disagree about whether a painting is beautiful, does this imply that one of you has poor judgment? Is beauty *in the eye of the beholder*, is it *in the thing itself*, or is it some combination of the two?

WRITE A "SCIENTIFIC" DESCRIPTION OF A PAINTING

Can art give us any knowledge? If so, what kind of knowledge does it give us? What if the only kind of knowledge art can give us must be expressed in terms of physics, chemistry and the other "hard sciences?" Find a reproduction of a painting you like, either one you own or a photo from an art book in the library. Focus on the painting as a physical object. If the book tells you how large the painting is, write those measurements down. List the colors used in the painting. If you have special knowledge of pigments, describe the pigments that the artist probably used for the painting. If the painting uses perspective, consider how the illusion of three dimensions is created. If you had time, you could go into how the painting is interpreted by the eye and brain.

Do you believe that such scientific knowledge is the only kind of knowledge to be gained from a work of art? Alfred Jules (A. J.) Ayer did not consider art to be cognitive; that is, there is no special artistic knowledge we can gain from a painting, sculpture or any other work of art. We can study it as a scientific object, examine its chemistry, physics and the technical details of how the work of art was made. We can study the biological processes that cause emotions that arise from works of art. We can even study the history of art through a work of art - Ayer believes that any language that can be verified by the senses can give us knowledge of the world. However, any special artistic knowledge cannot be evaluated by the senses. And emotion, Ayer believes, is not knowledge, and art in itself does not give us insight into the way the world is.

Do you agree with Ayer? Does the scientific description you gave of a work of art capture all it can tell us about the world, or is there anything we can learn about the world from a work of art that we cannot learn in any other way?

Thomas Aquinas would not have a problem with viewing a work of art in terms of science or history. However, he also believed that works of art, if well-crafted, can tell us truths about the world, truths that cannot be gained in any other way. Through good art, we contemplate beauty. A beautiful work of art, according to Aquinas, has a pleasing form that gives it unity (Aquinas calls this *integrity*). The parts of a work of art are related to each other in a well-ordered and beautiful way (Aquinas calls this *proportion*). And the best works of art clearly reveal the other two elements (Aquinas calls this *clarity*). Through these elements, we not only gain knowledge of a beautiful object, but through that object we know something of the beauty of the ultimate source of beauty, God. For Aquinas, the elements are not subjective; integrity, proportion and clarity are really *in* the work of art, and in that sense, the knowledge we gain from a work of art has its origin in sense experience.

Is Aquinas correct that a work of art gives us knowledge of beauty that we could not gain in any other way? Alternatively, is Ayer correct that though art can cause us to have strong emotions, the only knowledge we can gain from it is either scientific or historical and there is no special aesthetic knowledge?

GO TO A MUSEUM AND LOOK AT ABSTRACT ART

Although not all modern art is abstract, a great deal of it is. Have you heard people complain about abstract art? Perhaps they have seen a photo of an abstract painting in a book and commented, "I could do a better job if I spread out a canvas and threw around paint with my brush." Have you felt that way yourself? Have you walked by an abstract sculpture at a public building and thought, "This is not art?" Visit your local art museum and examine the abstract works. Do you believe that they are works of art? Is there something about their form that you admire, or do you think they do not belong in an art museum? Have you ever thought, "Some of these abstract paintings and sculptures do not look like art to me, but the people at the museum think they are, and what do I know? They're the experts, after all?"

George Dickie (1924-), who taught philosophy at the University of Illinois at Chicago, believes that the experts, the leaders of institutions such as art museums, art galleries, art critics, and other *insiders* in the art community, determine which works are considered to be art. (He also believes that works of art must be objects that have been made or altered by human beings - artifacts rather than natural objects). Dickie calls this insider's world *the artworld*, and his theory of art is called *the institutional theory of art*. Do you agree with Dickie? Are *the powers that be* in the *artworld* the only factor that determines what is art? Does reflecting on your experience in the art museum make you agree more or disagree more with Dickie? Why?

In his *formalist theory of art*, Clive Bell (1881-1964), a significant British art critic, agrees with Dickie that abstract art can be considered to be *art*. However, he also believes that is true only if the alleged work of art has *significant form*. *Significant form* is present when the lines and colors in a work of art are arranged in such a way that we feel a special emotion, an *aesthetic emotion*. The feeling is similar to what the artist feels when the artist appreciates the form in the work he has made.

When you visited the museum, did you appreciate the forms of the abstract paintings and sculptures you saw? Did a particular combination of lines, shapes, and colors move you to admire the overall structure? If so, this is evidence, according to Bell, that the work of art you admire has significant form. The form is in the work itself; it is not something imposed by the artistic community. Is Bell correct? Do you find Dickie's view more convincing? Do you disagree with both philosophers and believe that abstract art is not art at all?

CONSIDER A COLA CAN TO BE A WORK OF ART

Have you thought of ordinary objects as works of art? You may be familiar with Andy Warhol's use of Campbell's soup labels and other objects of our consumer culture in his art. What about a cola can? Find a can of any cola you choose and place it on display. You might set it on a block of wood or some other stand. You might invite your friends over and ask them whether your cola can is a work of art. What do you think they will say?

The French artist Marcel Duchamp (1887-1968) was one of the founders of *Dadaism*. *Dadaism* questioned traditional concepts of art and tended to be ironic, even humorous, in its attempts to redefine art. One of Duchamp's most famous works is *The Fountain*. *The Fountain* is a urinal without a pipe; on one side, it is signed, "R. Mutt 1917." Even though Duchamp did not mold the urinal, he did sign it with the humorous signature and place it on display. He was attacking the notion of a select few in an elite establishment determining the boundaries of art.

Do you believe that the process of displaying the urinal turns it into a piece of art? If so, what does this imply for the question of whether your cola can is a work of art? Is art something restricted to works specifically produced *as art*? Does putting an ordinary object on display and identifying it as a *work of art* make it a work of art? Can *found works*, or *readymades*, such as urinals or cola cans, be works of art in the same way that the *Mona Lisa* is considered to be a work of art?

Jacques Maritain (1882-1973) believed that attempts such as Duchamp's to *transmute* ordinary objects, such as urinals or cola cans, into works of art are flawed. According to Maritain, art is designed to truly illuminate things, not change them into something they are not. Calling a urinal or a cola can a *work of art* stretches the meaning of art to the breaking point, even if Duchamp means to be ironic or humorous. *The Fountain* is like a work of magic - by the force of his will Duchamp tried to magically transform an ordinary useful object into art. Maritain held that this makes art an intellectual exercise whereby we try to interpret the artist's secret code. Thus, scholars have argued not only about the meaning of Duchamp's urinal, but also about the meaning of Duchamp's signing the *sculpture* as "R. Mutt 1917." Maritain believes that such an intellectual approach to art ignores the creative vision an artist must have into reality, something that involves more than mere intellect.

Do you agree with Maritain? Does Duchamp subvert the true meaning of art in *The Fountain*? Do you believe Maritain's position on the nature of art is elitist? What do you think of the status of your cola can now? Do you now believe that it is a work of art?

PAUL GAUGUIN'S PAINTINGS AND HIS LIFE

Find some pictures of paintings by the French artist Paul Gauguin (1848-1903). You can find many on the Internet, and you can also check your local library. Pay special attention to the great art he painted while on Tahiti. Now read a biography of Gauguin. It could be a full-length biography or a short biography online, as long as it goes into his personal life. Read the details of how he treated his family, oftentimes leaving them destitute for the sake of his art. Given the great art he produced after he abandoned his family, do you believe his contribution to world of art makes up for his behavior?

The British philosopher Bernard Williams refers to the dilemma as *The Gauguin Problem*. Williams believed that a bad moral life, if it is for the sake of a higher cause such as producing great art, may be justified. Writers who leave their husbands or wives to focus on their writing and artists who ignore the needs of others to paint or sculpt would be in this category. Do you agree with Williams? Does producing great art justify an immoral life?

Aristotle believed that what makes a person good is having certain virtues, stable character traits that help a person do the right thing in a given situation. According to Aristotle, the right thing to do is a *middle way* between extremes; thus courage is a middle path between cowardliness and foolhardiness. However, there are some actions that are always wrong; among these are murder, theft and adultery. These actions never meet the mean, since they are always evil. There is no higher justification for such actions, whether the alleged justification be for the sake of art or any other *higher* cause.

Is Aristotle right that some actions are wholly wrong no matter what the circumstances? Assume that if Paul Gauguin had not left his family, his contribution to art would have been significantly less. Does this make any difference in your judgment of his actions? Why or why not?

LOOK AT YOUR PHOTO WHILE LISTENING TO MUSIC

Find a photo of yourself, preferably a formal photo. While examining it, play a piece of music which sounds triumphant, such as the main theme from *Star Wars*, and another piece of music which is ominous in tone, such as the Darth Vader theme from *The Empire Strikes Back*. If you prefer popular music, play a stirring song followed by a something like AC-DC's *Hell's Bells*. Is your attitude toward yourself in the photo affected by the type of music you play? Does the *Star Wars* theme make you seem more heroic, and the *Darth Vader* theme make you seem a shady figure? Suppose you play a classical piece followed by the hard-driving heavy metal piece of your choice. How does this change your attitude?

Now try looking at someone else while listening to music - a family member, a friend, a roommate. Does your companion appear as a swashbuckling hero if you play the opening *Star Wars* theme? If you play a sentimental piece such as Simon and Garfunkel's *Bridge over Troubled Water*, does this person appear to you more willing to help you through the worst times? If you hear the theme from a horror movie, such as *The Ring*, do you feel fearful as you gaze into your companion's face?

Does music have the power to change our attitudes and emotional responses to things and people? Plato thought so. He believed that such power is dangerous, a threat to the order of the state. Thus, he believed the government should strictly regulate the kinds of music allowed in the state. Philosophers called *expressionists* agree with Plato that the main effect of music is to move our feelings (although their attitude toward music usually is more positive than Plato's). Another group, the *formalists*, believe that what is really important in music is not expressing emotion, but the form of music (notes, rhythm, etc.). Does your experience with music lead you to support one of these views?

Does music change your (or another person's) character? If the *Darth Vader* theme leads you to imagine yourself or the person you're looking at as sinister, does that imply that you (or the other person) *are* sinister? Try this experiment with plants, animals and inanimate objects. Does the music you hear change the nature of the things you see, or is it only your mood toward people and things that changes? If so, how does your mood affect your perception?

If emotions change our perceptions of things, is it possible to totally separate our emotions from the way the world appears to us? Can we gain knowledge about someone or something through a particular emotion such as joy or fear? On the other hand, do emotions stirred by music detract from knowledge, or is our knowledge of a person or thing the same no matter what our emotional attitudes toward it might be?

Now look at your photo or your friend without listening to music. Is your experience of both any different than with the music?

GET TO KNOW A FICTIONAL CHARACTER

Have you ever become lost in a book you were reading? Have you sweated with a character as he runs from a fierce animal about to tear his flesh? Have you cried with a woman whose heart has been broken by a faithless husband? Do your favorite characters sometimes take on a life of their own? Do you ever feel that they might be real, living some place outside the author's imagination?

Find a book of fiction you have read before, one in which you were lost in the story and sympathetic with a particular character. Re-read the book. Try to get to *know* that character. Learn all you can about the character's appearance, personal habits and other nuances - those things that make someone a unique individual. Try to think what your character thinks; get inside her mind. Discover her favorite foods and drinks. Learn all about those she loves, her family and friends. Find out what she fears. Live with her as the story unfolds.

When you finish the book, how do you feel about your character? Has your attitude towards her changed in a positive or negative way? Engage your character in conversation; ask questions. Imagine her answers. Do you find that this deepens your understanding of the character? Are you beginning to think of her as real, perhaps more real than a stranger in the "actual" world? Often we may hear about people in the news, such as the president of the United States or a significant scientist and know very little about that individual as a person. Is it possible to *know* a fictional character better than a stranger in the real world?

Does getting to know your character give you insights into human nature? You may have found, in your experience with your family and friends that you have learned a great deal about the way people think, feel and behave. You may also have gained some insights into human nature, good or bad, in your encounters with strangers - store clerks, bank tellers, plumbers and so forth. Most of us probably know only a few people with such depth that we can know how they feel and think almost better than we know ourselves. While strangers may seem more like abstractions to us, people we know and love somehow can seem more real, more *concrete*, more *whole* than other people.

Is it possible that fictional characters, when well developed, can be, from your point of view, more *concrete*, more *whole*, more *human* than a mere acquaintance in the actual world? Louis Mackey (1926-2004), a philosopher who taught for many years at the University of Texas, thought so. He believed that if you read a nonfiction work that mentions a real person in passing, that individual is an abstraction to you. In a sense he does not seem real. However, a well-developed fictional character, to the reader, can be more of a *human being* than the person who actually lives in this world. Do you agree?

If it is true that a character can be more *real*, more *human* than a stranger or casual acquaintance, is it possible to have a relationship with that character that is, in some sense, *real?* The great Jewish existentialist philosopher Martin Buber distinguished between *I-It* and *I-Thou* relationships. If you have an *I-It* relationship with a person, you look on that individual as an object, a thing, rather than as a complete human being. That is not necessarily bad; if you go to the bank, you may think of the teller in terms of what she does rather than as a whole human being. It is not good, however, to treat your family members and friends as things. An *I-Thou* relationship is more intimate; you care for another person and know that individual in meaningful way. Do you think it could be possible to have an *I-Thou* relationship with a character in a novel? Do you think that your experience of getting to know your character created an *I-Thou* relationship?

WRITE A PARAGRAPH USING ONLY METAPHORS
AND OTHER FIGURES OF SPEECH

Try writing a paragraph that uses no *literal* language. You may use metaphors, similes and any other figure of speech you choose. When you are finished, read what you wrote.

Does your paragraph make sense? Do you think that another reader could make sense of it? Show the paragraph to a friend. Can the friend understand what you are saying? It is possible to have a complete language that uses only figures of speech? Does this language tell you more about the world or does it get in the way of knowing the world?

Now try playing a game with a friend or a small group of friends. In this game, each person is allowed to speak only using figures of speech. The only exception is that ordinary verbs can be used. How well do you communicate with each other? Is your use of figurative language clarifying or confusing?

Now write another paragraph, trying to avoid all figures of speech, and read the finished product. Were you successful in using words with literal meaning? Could any of the words also have figurative meaning? Is any meaning lost when you use only literal language? Are there insights about the world that you might gain using figurative language that you lose using only literal language?

Repeat the conversation experiment, using only literal language and avoiding all figures of speech. The conversation should continue for at least a half hour. Was it possible to communicate using only the *literal*? Is any meaning lost?

Owen Barfield (1898-1997) believed that originally it was not possible to distinguish the *literal* from the *figurative*, especially the *metaphorical*. Words such as *pneuma*, the Greek word for *air*, also meant *breath* and *spirit* and these meanings originally formed such a unity that the *literal* and *metaphorical* were merged. Over time, literal meaning arose from words that originally had metaphorical meaning as well. He believed that such language was an aid, rather than a hindrance, in helping us to understand the world. He believes that literal meaning tends to divide the wholeness of reality so that we only focus on parts.

If Barfield is correct, human beings at one time did speak (and perhaps write) using only what today would be called *figures of speech*. It would also follow that we lose insight into the world when we use literal language. Do you agree with Barfield? How do the results of your experiment in writing relate to your conclusion?

John Locke had a very different attitude toward figurative language than Barfield. Although Locke believed that figurative language could be used as *decoration*, only literal language could refer to *distinct ideas* and communicate knowledge about the world. In any speech or writing designed to give us knowledge, Locke believed figurative language should be avoided.

Looking back at the results of your experiments, do you believe that Barfield or Locke is correct? Is figurative language only decoration, or is its use unavoidable in our attempts to understand the world around us?

READ A STORY
THEN READ A BIOGRAPHY OF THE AUTHOR

Have you ever wondered about the lives of the authors of your favorite stories? Would knowing about an author's life change how you read a story? Read a favorite story. It might be a short story or novella; what is important is that it is a story you enjoy. Then find a biography of the author either at the library or online. Does any information about the author help you better understand the story? If so, what information? If not, do you believe that information about the author of a story is irrelevant for better understanding that story?

The French literary critic Roland Barthes (1915-1980) believed in what he labeled *the death of the author*. That is, he believed that information about an author's life, background, or intention for writing a work is irrelevant for understanding that work. Do you agree? Does the experience of reading a story and the author's biography affect your answer? How?

The French literary critic André Morize (1883-1957) believed that in order to understand a work of literature, a person has to understand the historical background of the work, the author's biography and the author's intention in writing the work. The idea is that a work of literature is written at a particular time from a particular person's perspective with a particular audience in mind. His approach to literature is sometimes called *traditional historicism* or *historical-biographical criticism*.

Is there merit to Morize's position? Did you notice any cultural references in the story or book you read that you failed to understand? If you noticed such references, did your reading of the author's biography clarify them? Can a story really stand on its own without any knowledge of the author's life? If not, how is this relevant to classic literature, such as the plays of Shakespeare or the books of the Bible, works of which we know little about the authors' lives? If someone read the story you enjoyed reading one hundred or two hundred years from now, would it help that person to better understand the work if she understood something about the author's life? If so, would such information matter more to a person in the far future than to you? Why?

HAVE A DIALOGUE WITH A STORY OR A BOOK

Read a story or book you enjoy. It can be in any genre: literary, romance, horror, science fiction, thriller, mystery. Pretend the author and characters are speaking to you and speak back to them. As you dialogue, do you find that the author had any expectations of you as a reader? That is, if you are reading a horror story or novel, does the author expect something that happened to a character to scare you? In a detective story, does the author expect you to try to solve the mystery? If a character does many evil things, do you expect the character to continue to do evil things?

What about your own expectations regarding the story? If you are reading horror, do you expect to be scared? Are you disappointed if you read what the author or publisher markets as horror and you are not scared? If you're reading what is stated to be fantasy, are you disappointed if the world of the story is too much like this world?

Jacques Derrida, a French philosopher, believed that there is no true meaning to a story. A story or novel means what the reader interprets it to mean, so that one reader could interpret it one way and another reader could interpret it an entirely different way. Applied to genre, one person could read a story as horror while another could read it as romance and there is no right answer to whether the story is a horror story or a romance. The same applies to other genres as well. In addition, different people my read the plot in entirely different ways, or interpret characters' actions in different ways. Each individual interpretation is equally valid. Do you think Derrida is right? Is whether a story is horror, romance or science fiction merely the interpretation of whoever reads it? Applied to the plot of a particular story, does how the plot develops set up expectations in the reader, or is this arbitrary? Or if a character is set up in a particular way, does the reader have expectations of the kinds of things the character will do next? Do you think the author also has expectations of how the reader will approach the plot and characters?

Umberto Eco (1932-), an Italian novelist, believes that there are limits to the meanings a story or book can have. He argues that there is an understood *contract* between author and reader so that the meaning arises from a combination of what the author wrote and what the reader expects. Applied to genre, people who read horror have certain expectations of what the story structure will be like. There will be frightening elements in the story, eerie elements that go beyond our ordinary understanding (even in serial killer novels the killer often has almost supernatural powers). Other expectations are set up by the plot and the way characters are developed. The author has his own expectations of what the reader will find in the story. Such expectations are partly subjective, but not wholly so.

Is Eco right? Is a story a kind of dialogue or *contract* between the author and reader? Given your experience of dialogue, do you believe Derrida or Eco to be closer to the truth? Why?

Read an Ancient Work of Literature

Can someone who wrote thousands of years ago still speak to us today? Or was the ancient world so different from ours that its writers have nothing to say to us? Read an ancient work of literature. It can be a Greek play such as Sophocles' *Oedipus Rex*, a dialogue of Plato such as *The Apology* or an epic poem such as the *Iliad* or the *Odyssey*. Were you able to understand the work? Did it say something meaningful to you? Now find at least two other people willing to read the same work. Let them express what meaning they found in the work. Were all the meanings the same?

Robert Penn Warren (1905-1989) was an American writer and literary critic, associated with the *New Criticism*. He believed that a literary work should be studied on its own merits as literature, without trying to determine the original motives of the author. Literature has value for what it reveals about universal human experience. While we should not ignore the historical background of a work of literature, that is not central for understanding the work. Ancient works of literature can illuminate human experience as well as medieval, modern or contemporary works. Through a careful study of the text, we can understand what ancient literature has to tell us, despite the cultural differences between the ancient and contemporary worlds.

Do you agree? When you read the ancient work, were you able to understand its message without reading the introduction or without using special aids such as dictionaries? Did you find the cultural gap between you and the ancient writer too large?

Hans-Georg Gadamer (1900-2002), a German philosopher, believed that the cultural gap between the writer of a work of literature and its readers is significant. This is true even of contemporary literature, but the gap is greater when we are dealing with ancient authors. One of the founders of *reader-response criticism*, Gadamer believed in the necessity of a *fusion of horizons* to understand a work of literature. That is, you, as a reader, must fuse your own background and beliefs with that of the writer of the literary work. In that way, you can gain meaning from the work. This means that another reader may find a different meaning in the work than you do. Was this the case in your experiment reading an ancient work with your friends? Even if different people find different meanings in a work of literature, can literature still communicate with us and give us insight into human experience? Why or why not?

WRITE A POEM USING TWO METHODS

Have you ever tried to write a poem? Have you read poems? Does poetry seem strange to you, like reading a foreign language, or do you feel at home when you are reading poetry? What about writing poetry? If you have tried it, is it something that comes easy to you? If you do write poetry, do you "let the spirit flow" and write the first items that come to your mind, or do you plan out a poem as you write? Perhaps you do both - if so, which do you think is the better method?

Write a poem, even if you have never written one before. First, write it without planning - just write the first words that come to mind, even if they do not seem to make sense. What results? Did you write a poem that you could understand? If you were unable to understand the poem, were you able to find some esoteric or strange meaning in it?

Now write another poem but plan out what you are going to write. Make notes, outline, and if you are going to use rhyme, plan out your rhyme scheme. Compare the result to the first poem you wrote. Which was better? Which version do you think best represents what poetry really is?

Richard Eberhart (1904-2005) was an American poet. He believed, following the philosopher Plato, that poetry was best written under a kind of *divine madness*. This is, when you have an overcharge of emotion that you must write down, write it down - it will probably be the best poem you can write at the time. He did not believe in revising these poems, for the overflow of emotion was sufficient to express best what the poet is trying to say.

If you can find a book of his poetry, read some of Eberhart's poems. Then read over your poem you wrote based on what first came to your mind. Do you think it is possible to write a good poem based on emotion, based on what comes into your mind in some *divine madness*? Or do you believe that you have to plan out a poem and carefully revise it to write a good poem?

The great Anglo-American poet Wystan Hugh (W. H.) Auden (1907-1973) carefully crafted and revised his poems constantly, to the point that editors tended to include earlier versions of his poems in collected editions of his poetry. His view was that if the poems did not reflect his world view at the time, they should be discarded or revised. He did not deny that poetry expresses emotion, but like the vast majority of poets, he believed that poems should be carefully crafted over a period of time.

Read some of Auden's poetry. Re-read the poem you carefully planned and crafted. Do you believe that craft and revision destroys the emotion of poetry, eliminating the *divine madness* that inspires it, or do you agree with Auden's approach of slow, careful use of craft and constant revision? If poetry is crafted slowly, what, then, is the nature of poetry?

FIND SOME FUNNY JOKES

When you laugh at joke, what is it about the joke that makes it funny? See if you can find out by reading a joke you find funny in a book of jokes or online, or watching a funny video or movie. Then analyze the jokes and ask yourself, "Why is this joke funny?" Have your friends read or hear the same jokes until they find one that you all agree is funny. Does their reasoning about why a joke is funny agree with yours?

The English philosopher Thomas Hobbes believed that humor is a way of making ourselves feel better at the expense of someone else. It is the feeling some people get when watching someone slip on a banana peel or watching a video of someone embarrass themselves in a silly skating or bicycle accident. The idea is that humor arises when you think, *I'm sure glad that person's not me, and I'm better off than he or she is!* Jokes often involve belittling a character in the joke or playing off some person's misfortune. Many jokes on late night television are based on a president's mistakes or clumsy language. So for Hobbes, jokes serve as ego boosters and help us to feel that we are better than other people.

Do you agree with Hobbes? Were the jokes you and your friends found funny jokes that played off someone else's misfortune? If so, were the jokes funny because you felt superior to that poor person in some way?

The Scottish philosopher Francis Hutcheson (1694-1746) disagreed with Hobbes. Humor does not arise from our sense of superiority over others. Rather, humor, including jokes, are funny due to *incongruity*. That is, the humor from a joke arises from a surprise, something unexpected, a *punch line*. Although this may not be the funniest joke in the world, it will serve as an example.

A man hires a sorcerer to keep zombies out of his house. His wife asks, "Why are you wasting money on a sorcerer. You know there aren't any zombies?" The man replies, "See. It works."

The expected answer is either for the man to say *Yes, there is such a thing as a zombie* or to say, *I guess it is silly.* Instead, he says something unexpected, incongruous, and from that humor arises.

Do you agree with Hutcheson? Were the jokes you and your friends found funny due to incongruity? Or is Hobbes correct? Did you find Hobbes correct for some jokes and Hutcheson correct for others? Could humor be more complex than either a feeling of superiority or incongruity?

WATCH A SAD MOVIE

D o you like to watch sad movies? If you do, what is it about them that you find appealing? If you do not, what is it that you dislike about them? Do you find it strange that some people enjoy watching sad movies?

Watch a sad movie. It could be something as sentimental as *Where the Red Fern Grows* or something more *intellectually sad* such as one of Ingmar Bergman's films. Did you feel sad? Did you cry? Was the experience a good one nonetheless, or did you find the experience negative, one that ruined the rest of your day?

Plato, the Greek philosopher who founded his school, *The Academy*, in Athens, Greece, obviously did not watch movies. However, he was familiar with plays and with poetry, which was usually read in public in his day. For Plato, works of art of any kind were dangerous. The first reason is that they are far from the real world, which for Plato was the world of the *Forms*. *Truth, Beauty, Good, Mathematical Laws*, and even *Dogness* and *Catness*, according to Plato, really exist in a world of their own separate from the world of our senses. The world of our senses participates or *copies* the world of the *Forms* but is not ultimately real. Although the world of our senses is not *illusion*, it is *illusory* if we confuse it with the real world. Since art is the copy of a copy, works of art, including plays and poems, are at the lowest level of reality. If Plato lived today, he would almost certainly say the same thing about movies.

Worse, plays and poems, as well as other works of art, stimulate dangerous emotions. Sadness can make someone despair, and anger can lead someone to commit crimes or rebel against the state. We should at all costs, if we wish to become wise, remove ourselves from the sources of such intense and destructive emotions. Today, that would include avoiding movies.

Is Plato correct? Did you find the sad movie harmful to you? Do you think that movies bring out undesirable emotions in people?

Plato's student, Aristotle, believed that plays and poems have a positive effect. Instead of encouraging us to have negative emotions, they purge negative emotions. When someone watches a sad play or reads a sad poem, he or she is able to get rid of those emotions in the theater or in the reading. Then those emotions cannot harm others, since they have already been *purged* (a process Aristotle calls *catharsis*). Aristotle would probably say the same thing about movies today - a sad movie can purge emotions of sadness from us, giving us a better outlook after the movie than before.

Was this your experience when you watched the sad movie? Was it helpful in purging sad feelings, or did it encourage you to continue to have sad feelings as Plato suggested?

FOR FURTHER LEARNING

I. Online Resources in Philosophy

Encyclopedias

Stanford Encyclopedia of Philosophy. At: http://plato.stanford.edu
Internet Encyclopedia of Philosophy. At: http://www.iep.utm.edu
A Dictionary of Philosophical Terms and Names. At:
http://www.philosophypages.com/dy/
Dictionary of Philosophy, edited by Dagobert D. Runes (1942). At:
http:// http://www.ditext.com/runes/h.html

Primary Sources

An excellent summary of links to primary sources in philosophy is
found at:
http://paideiacentre.ca/resources/research/philosophy

Free Course Material

A fine webpage with course materials from a variety of university
philosophy courses, including introductory courses, is found at:
http://www.skilledup.com/learn/openu/learn-philosophy-online-
free/

II. Print Resources in Philosophy

Dictionaries and Encyclopedias

Angeles, Peter A. and Erlich, Eugene. *HarperCollins Dictionary of
Philosophy: In-Depth Explanations and Examples Covering More Than 3,000
Entries.* 2nd edition. New York: HarperCollins, 1992. A clear, excellent
short dictionary of key philosophical terms and significant philosophers.

Edwards, Paul, editor. *The Encyclopedia of Philosophy.* New York:
Macmillan/Collier, 1972. A classic work, well worth exploring today. A
supplemental updated volume edited by Donald Borchert was published
by Macmillan in 2005.

Flew, Antony. *A Dictionary of Philosophy.* Revised 2nd edition. New
York: St. Martin's Griffin, 1984. A fine dictionary by a well-known
philosopher in the analytic tradition.

Honderich, Ted, editor. *The Oxford Guide to Philosophy.* 2nd edition.

Oxford: Oxford University Press, 2005. An excellent and scholarly dictionary with detailed articles.

Introductory Texts

The newest editions of university texts in philosophy are expensive; however, older editions can often be bought for little more than shipping charges.

Chaffee, John. *The Philosopher's Way: Thinking Critically about Profound Ideas.* Pearson/Prentice-Hall. This is the textbook I use in my own Introduction to Philosophy courses. It is a clear and has numerous integrated readings from primary sources, so that you get to read some Plato, Aristotle, Kant, and so forth.

Palmer, Donald. *Looking at Philosophy: The Unbearable Heaviness of Philosophy Made Lighter.* McGraw-Hill. Any edition is fine. Palmer is clear and uses comics to illuminate as well as for humor. Do not let that fool you - this is a thorough, excellent historical introduction to the field.

Stumpf, Samuel Enoch and Feiser, James. *Socrates to Sartre and Beyond: A History of Philosophy.* McGraw-Hill. Any edition from the last thirty years is fine. This is the best one-volume historical introduction to philosophy I have found.

Standard Multi-Volume Histories of Philosophy

Copleston, Frederick. *A History of Philosophy.* Several different publishers, with the number of volumes dependent on the publisher. This is the best secondary source multivolume history out there, and it takes a middle-of-the-road approach that gives the student what is needed. Father Copleston was a clear writer - if you can work through Copleston you will have an excellent understanding of philosophy's history and be ready to tackle primary sources.

Jones, W. T. *A History of Western Philosophy.* 5 volumes. Harcourt. This is another fine history with many integrated readings from primary sources. I recommend reading Copleston first, followed by Jones.

These sources are only a drop in the bucket from the vast field of philosophy - but they will keep you busy - and learning a wonderful field - for a long time.

INDEX OF NAMES

INDEX OF SUBJECTS

immortal, 3, 19, 99
inanimate object, 150
incongruity, 212, 213
indiscernibility of identicals, 48
individual, 11, 22, 31, 32, 42, 48,
 49, 56, 57, 61, 69, 74, 94, 132,
 134, 149, 187, 201, 202, 206
individuals, 8, 21, 94, 134, 169
Inductive reasoning, 130
infinite, 25, 26, 46, 100, 168
initial baptism, 49
integrity, 192
internal speaking, 88
Islam, 101
It's a Wonderful Life, 167, 168
I-Thou relationship, 146, 202
jokes, 212
Judaism, 101
knowledge, 4, 5, 11, 26, 28, 44,
 48, 52, 58, 77, 95, 96, 101, 102,
 110, 111, 112, 123, 129, 130,
 134, 149, 150, 151, 185, 192,
 193, 200, 204, 205
language, 6, 10, 33, 34, 37, 40, 56,
 70, 75, 76, 78, 79, 81, 88, 132,
 149, 150, 157, 159, 160, 163,
 164, 192, 203, 204, 210, 212
language game, 159, 163
language games, 158, 159
life, 3, 7, 9, 15, 16, 19, 20, 27, 28,
 33, 42, 43, 48, 49, 54, 57, 62,
 63, 67, 73, 75, 76, 84, 89, 93,
 97, 98, 99, 100, 107, 109, 133,
 134, 146, 149, 150, 163, 167,
 168, 171, 172, 173, 174, 177,
 179, 198, 201, 205
linguistic worlds, 157
literal, 30, 54, 203, 204
literature, v, 11, 208
lived body, 75, 76
logic, 4, 5, 10, 64

logical positivists, 10
love, 7, 15, 78, 79, 146, 150, 151,
 156, 157, 159, 171, 181, 182,
 183, 201
machine, 75, 76, 144
machines, 33, 131
magnet, iv, 117
marbles, 129, 130
material substances, 51
mathematics, 6, 25, 70, 129, 130,
 134
meaning, 3, 4, 6, 11, 12, 33, 34,
 82, 84, 97, 98, 101, 155, 156,
 157, 159, 160, 161, 168, 173,
 196, 197, 203, 206, 208, 210
meaningless, 10, 11, 97, 98, 168,
 185
medicine, 6, 76, 134
Medieval and Renaissance
 Philosophy, 8
memories, 15, 16, 44, 58, 129,
 132
mental contents, 78
mental image, 88, 135
mental state, 78
metaethics, 6
metanarrative, 155, 156
metaphorical, 203
metaphysical indeterminism, 112
metaphysics, iii, 4, 14
middle way, 198
mind, 4, 10, 12, 15, 16, 30, 40,
 48, 50, 57, 61, 73, 77, 81, 84,
 85, 86, 87, 88, 103, 113, 121,
 122, 128, 129, 131, 134, 135,
 138, 140, 141, 147, 149, 150,
 167, 169, 173, 174, 201, 205,
 210
mind-stuff, 57
mirage, 23, 24
mirror, 21, 133, 134

Made in the USA
Charleston, SC
21 December 2015